STARTING RIGHT

Books by Suzy Prudden:

Suzy Prudden's Creative Fitness for Baby and Child
Suzy Prudden's Family Fitness Book
See How They Run
Suzy Prudden's Fit for Life
Suzy Prudden's Spot Reducing Book
Suzy Prudden's Pregnancy and Back to Shape Book
Suzy Prudden's I Can Exercise Anywhere Book
Suzy Prudden's Exercise Program for Young Children

STARTING RIGHT

SUZY PRUDDEN'S FITNESS PROGRAM FOR CHILDREN 5–11

Suzy Prudden
and
Joan Meijer-Hirschland

Photographs by Nancy De Pra

Doubleday
NEW YORK LONDON TORONTO SYDNEY AUCKLAND

Published by Doubleday, a division of Bantam Doubleday Dell
Publishing Group, Inc., 666 Fifth Avenue, New York, New York 10103.

Doubleday and the portrayal of an anchor with a dolphin are
trademarks of Doubleday, a division of Bantam Doubleday Dell
Publishing Group, Inc.

Library of Congress Cataloging-in-Publication Data

Prudden, Suzy.
Starting right.

1. Physical fitness for children. 2. Exercise for
children. I. Meijer-Hirschland, Joan. II. Title.
RJ133.P792   1987   613.7′042   87-586

ISBN: 0-385-23635-2

To Jonathan Goldhill,
Whose love I have treasured and whom I have adored.

To Rita Silverman,
Anchor in every storm, thank you for your friendship, love, and support.

To my mother, Bonnie Prudden, my son, Rob Sussman, and my sister, Petie,
All of you teachers and dear friends. I am honored and grateful you are my family and that we are able to love each other "as we are" and not just as we'd like us to be.

Suzy Prudden

I wish to dedicate this book to my children, Peter, Richard, and Jackey Meijer. It's always amazing to me how patient children can be, and how sustaining their love is.

And to Hans Meijer, my dearest friend.

And to Bonnie Prudden, our mother. A very tough act to follow and a real inspiration.

Joan Meijer-Hirschland

ACKNOWLEDGMENTS

We would very much like to thank Adam Halperin, Karen Halperin, Oro Okore, Regina Schaffer-Goldman, Kevin Silverman, Jamie Wallace, Jennifer Wallace, Melissa Lem, Sophia Bernhardt, Doris Bernhardt, Simone Delerme, Jerry Delerme, Mariel Speier, Eric Speier, Graham Speier, ARon Weiss, and Jackie Meijer for their tireless posing and continued good sportsmanship during the long hours of picture taking.

We would like to thank Coach Lou Gallo and the staff and students in Rye, New York, Bob Stauderman and the staff and students in Poughkeepsie, New York, and Cinder Soule and her students in Bethel, Vermont.

We would also like to thank the Walden School Discovery Program in New York City, and Walden students Illana Shatz, Jessica Leader, Amanda Leader, Elizabeth Ceisler, Elizabeth Carmany, Janna Gordon-Elliott, Catherine Bushell, Alison Miller, Lea Landowne, Christine Wright, and Piper Weiss for taking class time to participate in the creation of this book and for doing it so well.

Finally we would like to thank Amy Allen, friend and neighbor, without whose generous and timely help this book could not have gotten finished.

Cover clothing for Suzy Prudden by Capezio Ballet Makers.
Cover clothing for children supplied by Morris Brothers of New York.

Contents

Introduction

WHERE IT ALL BEGAN

In the early 1950s our mother, Bonnie Prudden, ran an exercise school in the Knights of Columbus Hall in Harrison, New York. She had started the school in 1945 because she was a concerned parent who was also a skilled dancer and talented teacher. She did not start her school because she had a foreknowledge that without it we wouldn't have had a chance to develop strong, flexible, and well-coordinated bodies. Nor did she start it because she knew that there was something wrong with physical education in America. All that came later.

The exercise school was a good one and very popular. By the early 1950s it had grown from an original enrollment of twenty friends to a student body of hundreds, ranging in age from three to eighty-three. Bonnie felt that her program was making a difference to her own children and to her students, but she had no way of measuring the difference. She began looking around for an existing national or international test to see how her program stacked up against others.

By chance, she went rock climbing on weekends with Dr. Hans Kraus, a specialist in sports medicine with a real interest in back injuries and chronic back pain. Dr. Kraus was associated with Columbia-Presbyterian Hospital (now Columbia-Presbyterian Medical Center) in New York City and was a codirector of the Back Wellness Clinic for Columbia-Presbyterian. Bonnie asked Dr. Kraus if he knew of any test that she could use to measure the level of fitness of her pupils and the effectiveness of her program.

The only test that he knew was one he had developed in the course of his work with patients complaining of chronic back pain. Dr. Kraus and his associate, Dr. Sonya Weber, had discovered that 80 percent of the patients who came to the clinic seeking treatment for low back pain could not attribute their pain to pathological causes. Over the years they had discovered that these patients were simply lacking in basic strength and flexibility. For these patients radical treatments such as surgery and braces were not necessary. Bringing them up to a measurable point of strength and flexibility would cure the back pain.

Over the years of painstaking research they developed a bottom-line-level measurement for strength and flexibility: *the Kraus-Weber Minimum Muscular Fitness Test.* Consistently, when those suffering from nonpathological back pain achieved the level of physical strength and flexibility sufficient to pass the test, their pain would disappear. Just as consistently, if they allowed their strength and flexibility to drop to a point at which they failed the test, the back pain returned.

The following is the test that Dr. Kraus and Dr. Weber determined was the minimum level at which humans could live without chronic low back pain, the Kraus-Weber Minimum Muscular Fitness Test (this test is described in more detail on pages 12–17):

- Do one sit-up, legs straight, hands behind neck, someone holding down feet.
- Do one sit-up, knees bent, hands behind neck, someone holding down feet.
- While lying on back, raise and hold straight legs ten inches off floor for ten seconds.
- While lying on stomach, pillow placed under hips, with someone holding legs down, lift head, chest, shoulders, and arms off floor for ten seconds.
- While lying on stomach, pillow placed under hips, with someone holding down chest, lift straight legs off floor for ten seconds.
- Stand with feet together and legs straight and touch the floor; hold for three seconds.

Bonnie gave her students the Kraus-Weber Minimum Muscular Fitness Test in the spring of 1952. Since her students had been exercising their muscles all winter, it was not surprising that they passed the test with ease. The next fall, however, new students who had never taken an exercise class before were among the students taking Kraus-Weber for the first time. To Bonnie's surprise a significant number of these students failed.

Bonnie called Drs. Kraus and Weber and told them about the failures. They couldn't believe it. It had to be a fluke.

There were several things that made a child's failing the K-W Test highly significant and undesirable. Up until that time it had been assumed that children exercised themselves, and that in the course of climbing up and down and learning to walk and run, they automatically developed strong and flexible bodies. No one had dreamed that a child could fail a minimum test.

If children did fail that test, given that it was believed that they were naturally strong and flexible, what did that say about the validity of the test? Was the test too hard? Did it measure the minimum level of fitness, or was the standard too high? Was Drs. Kraus and Weber's work based on a faulty premise? What would that mean in terms of their years of painstaking research?

On the other hand, if the test did measure the minimum level and large numbers of children failed, what was happening to America's children? What would happen to future generations of American's?*

At that point no one knew any of these answers. They weren't even sure they had a question. They only knew that a number of the children who had come into Bonnie's school that fall couldn't pass the test.

Bonnie and Dr. Kraus determined to look further. They postulated four questions:

1. Was there a problem?
2. If there was a problem, was it an American problem or a worldwide problem?
3. If it was an American problem, how extensive was it?
4. If the problem was worldwide, was something wrong with the test?

Bonnie arranged with the city of Rye, New York, to test all the children in its school system (see Appendix C). The result of the testing showed that 56 percent of all the children in this wealthy suburban town failed the Kraus-Weber Minimum Muscular Fitness Test. *That first test group proved beyond a shadow of a doubt that there was a problem.*

The test results also showed that children graduating from high school failed with as high a percentage rate as children coming into school for the first time. *This suggested that school physical education programs were not meeting the physical needs of the students.*

Bonnie next tested in the city of Poughkeepsie, New York, with similar results: 58 percent of the student body failed. She then tested in Bethel, Vermont. Bethel is a very small rural village tucked into the hills of central Vermont. In Bethel, Bonnie found the first major difference in test results for an American population. Only 26 percent of

---

* Note: In point of fact, 47 percent of today's adults complain of chronic low back pain. Low back pain presently costs American industry $6 billion a year.

Bethel's children failed the test. *These findings suggested that the failures might be lifestyle-related.*

In Bethel, the lifestyle of the children was generally more active. At that time many of the kids still worked on their family farms. Walking was a way of life if they wanted to get from one place to another. Walking was generally up- and downhill. Unlike Rye and Poughkeepsie, Bethel had no school physical education program. It appeared to Bonnie that simply because of the way they lived, these kids came into school fitter and stayed fitter. (It is interesting to note some thirty years later, as the lifestyle of Bethel has changed and the children are not as physically active at home, they are entering school with a failure rate of 50 percent. These findings are still better than in the urban and suburban areas, but much worse than they were thirty years ago.)

Bonnie and Dr. Kraus spent the next summer testing in Austria, Italy, and Switzerland. The failure rate in Europe, ten years after the devastation of World War II when Europe was still in the middle of recovery, was 6 percent in Italy, 8 percent in Switzerland, and 8 percent in Austria.

Bonnie and Dr. Kraus next tested in Guatemala. Their test subjects were children who were in a hospital recovering from the effects of disease. These children failed only at 20 percent, some 36 points better than their healthy American counterparts.

That same year a colleague tested in Japan, another country suffering from the aftermath of war. There the failure rate was 12 percent.

The problem was definitely with the American population and not with the test. The problem appeared to be extensive.

Testing became a major part of the family life in the Prudden household. Bonnie tested everywhere she could find people willing to lie down. She tested in reform schools; she tested in posh boarding schools; she tested in the country; she tested in the city; she tested, and she tested, and she tested. The results were dismally the same.

From the results of her testing Bonnie concluded that the lifestyle of America's children was not conducive to the development of strong bodies. And because physical education departments were concentrating on games to the exclusion of general conditioning, they did not help children develop good exercise habits or strong bodies. As long as this was how school physical education programs were run (in many areas this is still how they are run), America's children hadn't a chance of developing strong bodies in school.

In July of 1956 the President's Citizens Advisory Committee (now known as the President's Council on Physical Fitness and Sports) was appointed, and 119 citizens, under the direction of Dr. Shane MacCarthy, began to wrestle with ways to address the problem. That they are still wrestling with the ways to address the problem thirty years later proves how difficult this problem is to solve.

WHAT DO TEST SCORES SHOW THIRTY YEARS LATER?

In 1984 a study was conducted on 18,857 boys and girls, ages 6 to 17. The test, which is much more inclusive than Kraus-Weber, was conducted in 57 high school districts and in 187 schools. It was the largest study of its kind ever undertaken in the United States. Some of the findings may be a little shocking to parents, nine out of ten of whom believe their children are fit.

- 98 percent of all children tested had at least one risk factor for heart disease; 38 percent had more than one risk factor. (Since risk factors multiply and square—they don't add—in their effects on victims, that is a very serious finding.)
- 40 percent of boys ages 6 to 12 could not do more than one pull-up; one out of four could not do any.
- 70 percent of all girls tested could not do more than one pull-up; 55 percent could not do any.
- 45 percent of all boys 6 to 14 and 55 percent of the girls could not hold their chin over a raised bar for more than 10 seconds.
- In the 50-yard dash, the girls in 1985 were significantly slower than they had been in 1975.
- In the simple flexibility sit test, 40 percent of the boys ages 6 to 15 could not reach beyond their toes (we found that statistic to be much worse with the standing flexibility test).
- Approximately 50 percent of the girls 6 to 17 and 30 percent of the boys 6 to 12 could not run a mile in less than 10 minutes (it's normal to walk a mile in 12 to 15 minutes).

In only 36 percent of the schools in America are children getting exercise sufficient for effective cardio(heart)-respiratory(breathing) function. In only 36 percent of the schools in America are children receiving daily physical education. In many schools, even where two hours a week are mandated, half an hour a week is the norm—and that includes changing and attendance time. The rest of the program is "covered" by expanded recess, or by the classroom teacher, who may or may not be able to teach exercise at all.

The major operational misunderstanding that is causing the problem in school is games.

At one time it was thought that winning teams meant a good overall physical education for everyone. Despite overwhelming evidence to the contrary, in people's minds games were and are the answer to children's need for exercise. All training in schools, colleges, and universities that train coaches was, and to some extent still is, focused on teams and games. Winning teams are NOT the measure of the effectiveness of a physical education program. Winning teams mean only that the already good athlete is getting good training. That's all they mean. Winning teams say nothing about the overall fitness of the student body. Cheering from the sidelines is not an aerobic activity.

The stress on games to the exclusion of exercise was a problem thirty years ago when Bonnie first brought her findings to the attention of the American public, and it remains the problem in most schools and communities today. This situation has to change. Until it changes, we will continue to have some of the poorest scores and highest failures in physical fitness in the world (right now we rank twenty-fourth in fitness, somewhere after Thailand).

We're not advocating the exclusion of games. We're saying don't exclude exercise in order to have games. We must get our kids exercising. We have to build good, simple, viable aerobic programs in the schools *to support the games.* We have to put in strong flexibility programs. We have to build strength for at least the core muscles, and we have to enhance balance and coordination.

This book is called *Starting Right.* That's the answer. First start by getting fit for games. Then play them with quality. First start by getting fit for life, then live it with quality.

STARTING RIGHT

1

Why This Book? The Growth Process

FIVE TO ELEVEN, THE FORGOTTEN YEARS

Where physical fitness is concerned, for many children, the ages five to eleven seem to have become the forgotten years. We don't know exactly why this group gets shortchanged, but everything we've seen and read seems to point that way. Younger children get lots of attention because parents want to be sure they get the "best possible start." Teenagers are easier to teach, and it's clear that they need programs. But those middle years get lost.

It seems as if parents believe that because their children have energy, they are naturally fit. Maybe the thought is that school-age children, once they've gotten that early good start, will carry the ball themselves. It may be that parents believe that school programs meet their children's needs. It may be that parents don't think their children can do as much as they really can between five and eleven. It may be that nobody really cares, that the struggle to make it is too hard and parents feel they can't do everything. Fitness is just too difficult along with everything else.

Whatever the underlying reason that is causing the problem, we want you to know that for the most part *your kids aren't getting fit by themselves.* We want you to know that fitness is tremendously important. Fitness may prove to be the motivator for better marks, the creator of discipline, the thing that makes other things possible. It isn't a back-burner item.

This book is a fitness program. All you have to do is introduce any part of it to your child and the program should help him—or her—get fit. Start with the Five-Mile Club (see "Aerobic Exercise Clubs" on page 137), or go to the Optimum Test and fitness program on page 17. Introduce the A, B, C, and D program a month before his favorite sport begins as a specific conditioning agent, and then keep him at it through that season and on to the next.

Many parents don't realize how capable their children are. As a start, we thought we would let you know what your children should be capable of doing, age group by age group, so that you can push ahead, introducing new sports into their lives as soon as it is possible to do so.

FIVE TO ELEVEN IN GENERAL

Five to eleven is the time by which kids have soaked up the knowledge needed for them to become functional human beings and are starting to prepare themselves to become adults. Five to eleven is an easy time to teach children new skills. Their bodies are malleable, and they have fewer bad habits to undo. Five to eleven might be regarded as the optimum window of opportunity for getting kids interested in sports as a way of life and for keeping them out of trouble in adolescence. Age ten, in particular, should be regarded as the time by which athletic interest should be established. Eleven can be such a fall-apart year that what you didn't start at ten you may not be able to start at eleven. And it's almost impossible to start as a teenager.

A great many wonderful changes go on in the years five to eleven. The changes don't appear to be as dramatic as those from birth to five, but they are, nonetheless. This is a preview period, one of the first major opportunities to see what your little person might become as an adult. And given some of the behaviors of adolescence, it's a good thing we have the preview so we know what's possible on the other side.

THE FIVE-YEAR-OLD

Your five-year-old probably still cannot throw a ball without kicking out at the same time, and he will often catch a ball with his arms rather than just his hands. He may be trying to introduce hand catching into his movement vocabulary and that might be a little frustrating. Beach balls are good to use with this group because they're slower than any other kind of ball, they're designed to allow your child to catch with his arms without feeling like a "baby," and they can be much less frustrating than smaller, heavier, more compact balls.

Your five-year-old's eyes and head now move almost simultaneously, rather than independently, which greatly improves coordination. He has a direct approach to most things; it's still going to be a little while before side approaches can be introduced with ease (e.g., batting a ball). He has greater control of general body activity. His gross motor skills (control of large muscles) are well developed, but small motor skills are not. While he may appear to you to be as capable as an adult in eye-hand coordination, he actually has quite a way to go with the finer patterns of development. So if there are things he can't do, it's often age-related; don't worry.

He is probably a demon on his tricycle, and biking may be one of his great loves. He's a big climber and big lifter. He may begin to be interested in things such as pogo sticks, stilts, and roller skates, but he's usually not too skillful with them and doesn't have much stamina. He can ski, horseback-ride, skate, swim, and hike.

Some fears regarding physical activities may appear. To support your child through these fears, listen carefully to what he's saying. Then, bit by bit, show him that he can go beyond what he thinks is his limit. It's important not to belittle these fears; they're real to your child.

Conversely, he may not be afraid when you are. The trick is not to let on that you're afraid, but to position yourself so that you can help him if he gets into trouble. You don't want to teach him fear if he hasn't got it.

Exercise periods for the five-year-old should include a variety of short bursts of activity. We recommend three-to-five-minute routines to music. Kids at this age love to march to music. They also like to jump to it, swing their arms to it, and even do sit-ups to it. Exercising to music is a painless way to introduce discipline to the body. We suggest you do as much to music as you can. That could include skiing and batting balls, as well as the exercises outlined in this book.

THE SIX-YEAR-OLD

Your child at six is undergoing a period of profound development in the underlying nervous system. These changes are substantial. Your child is experiencing new impulses across the board: new skills, new teeth, and lots of growth. It isn't easy.

The six-year-old is much more physical than he's ever been before. He likes active, almost rowdy games, such as tag, dancing, and climbing. He also loves to build and stack things, and this is a good time for introducing objects to enhance eye-hand coordination (jacks and any of the pat-a-cake variations starting on page 126).

Your child is like a whirling dervish, constantly in motion. He seems to approach activities with greater abandon than ever before. He's boisterous and likes ramble-scramble play, he's a bit of a menace when he plays indoors, and he loves physical experimentation. Tumbling, acrobatics, and ring and trapeze work generally improve. In addition to the programs in this book, skiing, riding, swimming, hiking, ice skating, and any of the individual sports that use gross motor skills are good to start now. Six-year-olds are so good they often make adults feel inferior. (Ever been deflated on a crowded ski slope as the peanut brigade whooshes past you?)

This is a great time to take up dancing lessons. For the child who isn't interested in dancing, karate and gymnastics are good substitutes.

Your six-year-old may appear fearless to the point of terrifying you. We can't agree on whether or not he's sensible about his own well-being, but between us we have four healthy children to prove that they generally survive. This is an important time for learning the difference between beneficial limit pushing and being out of control. It's a very hard time for parents. It is up to them to strike a balance between safety and curiosity, growth and inhibition.

Your six-year-old now has much more balance and freedom of movement. His gross motor activities are pretty much in hand and small motor activity is improving. He may be catching the ball with his hands more often and throwing in a more coordinated manner. He may be willing to take up tennis, though it may still be much too frustrating. This may depend on how patient the parent/teacher is willing to be. If your child's having a hard time, try a Nerf basketball to practice on if you really want him learning these batting-racket skills.

The key to handling your six-year-old is to let him push his limits and to provide lots of room for failure. Failure is the first step to success and must not be looked upon as bad or wrong. Failure is a most important part of learning and an opportunity for growth.

THE SEVEN-YEAR-OLD

Your seven-year-old may have a new orientation to the side position and can now learn about batting a ball and shooting a bow and arrow. His catching is much improved. He has more stamina than he had last year. It's good to keep up the aerobic conditioning routines demonstrated in this book. Flexibility is becoming more and more important because the child is spending a lot more time sitting than he did when he was younger, so be sure to emphasize the flexibility exercises, particularly for the boys. Swimming, skiing, horseback riding, karate, and dance lessons all become more and more enjoyable.

THE EIGHT-YEAR-OLD

Eight is a wonderful age for both you and your child. These kids are looking for new worlds to conquer. They like drama and rhythms and are fluid, graceful, and poised. They walk with a new freedom. Courage and daring are part of their makeup. It is an excellent time to teach them things about safety and first aid.

Your eight-year-old is healthier, speedier, and more open and skillful than he was before. He has more stamina, is increasingly fond of the rough and tumble, and enjoys himself much more than he did at seven. This child is a good observer and an active doer. He's lots of fun to be around, but may be especially hypersensitive to criticism. At eight, children's feelings are easily hurt. It is better to approach children with positive feedback than to point out their faults (actually, that's true for all of us). A positive correction might sound like this: "That was great! Now let's make it even better."

At eight, children like to play real games and can undertake much more complicated activities. They like team sports; it's soccer and baseball time. Just remember that, while soccer and basketball (boys' rules) might be a good way to get fit, baseball, which requires lots of standing around, isn't. The programs outlined in this book must be maintained for fitness—fitness for sports as well as for lifestyle.

At eight, possibly for the first time, some differentiation may be appearing in sex roles. This must *not* be tolerated, especially in sports. Boys and girls may seem to want to herd together and to treat the other group with disdain. If this is allowed, the girls will separate into girls' activities and the boys into boys' activities. This will be very bad for both sexes. They will each miss something important for their total growth.

THE NINE-YEAR-OLD

Nine is the best age for introducing or perfecting your child's sports skills. If you can get him involved in sports by nine or ten, you've probably got him involved through adolescence. Indeed, if you want your child involved in sports and you haven't gotten him involved by nine or ten, you may have to wait for adulthood.

Your child at nine has great interest in games and team sports and in learning to master his performance. He works hard and plays hard. He is interested in his own strength, but he doesn't know how to gauge his limits. He may even overdo. He's skillful in motor responses, knows it, and likes to show it. He's experiencing a lot of gratification because his timing is now more under control. He will tend to be very interested in competitive sports, fighting, and wrestling. He may be a bit timid about speed; be grateful. Your nine-year-old can pretty much do whatever sport he wants to do (with the possible exception of tackle football). The exercises in the program chapter of this book will keep him fit enough to do so.

One thing that may come up at this age is fear. The fact that a young rider trusts his horse or a young gymnast trusts his coach, and in the process does some incredible things, should not be interpreted as fearlessness. It may look as if your child hasn't a nerve in his body. That's simply not true. You may run into episodes of fear when changing horses or coaches, or almost anything else. They are something to watch for, heed, and consciously work through. Don't push! Such fear is very real to your child and should be overcome gently.

THE TEN-YEAR-OLD

Your ten-year-old is in the "athletic age." If you're going to get your child interested in sports, dance, or movement of any kind, don't wait. This is the optimum time to do it before adolescence. It may be the last time to do it before adolescence.

Children at ten love groups. A sports club, a dance program, or a karate school will channel their need to be members of a group in a positive direction.

You can see some real sexual differentiation at ten that was not evident before. The girls are forging ahead to maturity. There is a slight softening and rounding of the hips, a waist may be emerging, and the chest begins to grow. Arms become rounded, and the face begins to take on an oval shape, becoming less sharp and elfin.

This is the brink of the growth spurt for many girls. They may feel a soreness and tingling in the nipple region, and some girls may have developed breasts and pubic hair and may even be menstruating. This should not curtail fitness activities. To instill the belief that menstruation automatically causes cramps, or that girls have to be sick or helpless or stay in bed during their period, is to do them a great disservice. If you were programmed to believe that girls have to suffer through their periods, try not to pass on that information to your daughters. You can stop misinformation with yourself. You can be part of the last generation to be misled in that way.

THE ELEVEN-YEAR-OLD

Eleven is an age marked by mood swings and visible onset of immaturity in a whole new emotional way. It is the beginning of tremendous changes that involve the whole body. Eleven is your first taste of your child's adolescence and it's a shocker.

Your eleven-year-old sees his faults easily and his good qualities almost not at all. Positive reinforcement is important here, and fitness is one of the best reinforcements there is. You want this time to be as easy as possible for your child. And although it may not seem so, eleven is harder on him than on you.

This may be the last age where you have any real input. Make use of it!

2

What Is Fitness?

Fitness means preparedness. Fitness means that a person has prepared his body, through the performance of certain programs of exercise, to respond to most of the demands he makes on that body. Being fit does not require pushing and driving to become an Olympic-level athlete. Simply stated, fitness is the foundation of healthy living. It is a foundation for sports enjoyment and achievement.

We give our children a better quality of life if we start them developing patterns of fitness early. By showing them how much fun being fit and successfully participating in sports can be, we start them right.

Overall Fitness Is Comprised of Four Major Components:

1. ENDURANCE   It's impossible to talk about endurance without also talking about aerobics and cardiovascular fitness, because they're linked. In order to understand more about this, we have to look at what aerobic exercise is.

"Aerobic" means "living in air" or "utilizing oxygen." When your child sits at his desk in school and breathes normally, he's in an aerobic state. The amount of oxygen he's taking in and the amount of oxygen his body is using are in balance.

As he begins to exercise, however, his body begins to require more oxygen. As a result, his rate of breathing increases and his heart pumps faster to supply that extra oxygen need. He can stay in an aerobic state during exercise as long as he maintains a proper balance between his oxygen intake and his output of bodily energy. If he does not maintain that balance and exercises too hard, he becomes anaerobic. This means that his body begins to use more oxygen than he can take in and circulate to the muscles. Exhaustion and pain quickly follow.

Aerobic exercises are designed to increase breathing capacity and heart rates for a relatively long period of time without disturbing the balance between intake and use of oxygen. Running, swimming, cycling, walking, and dancing are examples of aerobic exercises. We have included an aerobic exercise program in this book, which begins on page 136.

Aerobic exercises performed regularly over a long period of time produce a *training effect.* This training effect puts the body in better shape and increases a person's capacity to do increasingly strenuous exercise. One of the beneficial results is a fitter cardiovascular system and greater protection from heart disease.

2. STRENGTH   There are two kinds of strength exercise: isometric and isotonic. An *isometric exercise* is one that uses the body's resistance against itself to strengthen the body. Isometric exercises simply tighten muscles. They can be used for some forms of prerelaxation exercise. Isometric exercises are excellent subtle exercises. They can be done in a crowded room, and no one will notice. They don't have application in flexibility, endurance, cardiovascular health, or coordination; all those are addressed by isotonic exercises.

A good isometric exercise you can teach your child is to pull in his stomach as tightly as he can and hold for ten seconds (tell him to be sure to keep breathing normally). He can perform this exercise right at his desk if he gets restless from too much sitting.

An *isotonic exercise* is one that uses body movements to strengthen the body. Isotonic exercises utilize a full range of motion. They enhance strength, flexibility, coordination, and endurance. They can be performed with or without weights and with or without resistance. Only through an isotonic exercise can you increase flexibility.

Examples of good isotonic exercises are simply running around the room waving your arms, and just about every exercise mentioned in this book. The strength exercises in this book are all isotonic.

The Five-to-Eleven-Year-Old and Weight Lifting to Build Bulk

This is a very important piece of information. A five-to-eleven-year-old cannot add bulk. Rambo is out until puberty. Weight lifting to overcome the perceived ninety-seven-pound-weakling syndrome doesn't work with him. It takes the chemical release of certain enzymes to add bulk. These enzymes don't yet exist in your child's body. Your child can become strong, but the strength will not make him look like Sylvester Stallone. Using the programs in this book will make your child strong. As things such as sit-ups and pull-ups become easier and easier, he can increase the number of repetitions and can increase the weights he uses. Do not confuse strength with bulk.

Do not confuse overweight with muscle. The ideal five-to-eleven-year-old body is lean. The skinny kid is the ideal kid and he should be told that every day.

Do Not Encourage Going for the Burn

It is very important in strength exercises not to "go for the burn." The body has only one way to tell you it's going too far, and that is to complain through pain. People can do permanent damage if they don't listen to their bodies. There is a possibility that minuscule tears can happen in muscles that are forced. The result can be structural weakening and eventually real trouble. It isn't an accident that sports medicine is one of the fastest-growing medical specialties in America, or that it didn't exist as a widespread medical specialty before the popularization of jogging and high-impact aerobics.

Teaching a program of sensible, moderate, and regular exercise, with a focus on sports preparedness, is what we recommend. That's what these strength exercises are designed to accomplish.

A Quick Word About Girls and Strength

There is a widely held assumption that girls are weak and that somehow that's a good, feminine thing to be. The assumption that women are weaker than men kept women from taking care of their own needs for years. Women simply forgot that their female predecessors walked from New York to California. It wasn't with soft muscles that they helped build this nation. Although we have only Founding Fathers in America, the men couldn't have done it by themselves. Today there are women bodybuilders (something that was unheard of in the 1950s), women paramedics, women bricklayers, women carpenters, women astronauts, women soldiers, women police officers, women fire fighters. So we know that women can be strong. We also know that muscles make the body defined and beautiful.

In the 1950s it was widely held that muscles would make women look ugly. Just look at Raquel Welch and see how ugly her muscles make her look. Hollywood beauties keep their bodies in excellent shape. They do so for two reasons: first, of course, because it's what makes the curves happen, and second, because being a movie actress is work! It is physically active work, the hours are long and hard, and the good roles are demanding both physically and mentally. Actresses and actors keep in shape for the same reason we all should: to be able to live our lives healthily.

3. COORDINATION Everything we do from getting out of bed in the morning to brushing our teeth at night takes coordination. Build ing endurance and strength in the body is only part of the picture. Children must learn how to use their endurance and strength in a smooth and coordinated manner.

Awkwardness is caused by an inability to coordinate movement. Children who are awkward are uncomfortable with their bodies. This results in discomfort with themselves, especially in social situations. By patterning movements and using music, moving from one exercise to another without taking a break, you teach your child how to use his body in a coordinated manner.

Full-body coordination exercises include combining activities: running while dribbling a ball, jumping rope, playing leapfrog. These are all examples of exercises that contribute to coordination. On the simple side, walking two or four steps with toes turned out and then walking two or four steps with toes turned in increases coordination.

Eye-Hand Coordination

Eye-hand coordination occurs when the brain instantaneously interprets signals from the eyes to the muscles in a way that allows coordinated movement and accuracy in connecting with an object. Eye-hand coordination is the underpinning for success in most games and for almost everything else you do in life. We see it in activities such as throwing darts, pitching, batting, kicking a ball, and catching. It's not quite so obvious in eating, sitting down in a chair without looking first, or writing. Although not manifested in a physical hand movement, even reading and organizing thoughts use the same eye-hand coordination process. As you increase a child's physical ability with eye-hand coordination exercises, you also increase his intellect.

There are a number of old-fashioned games that address eye-hand coordination which might not seem as valuable in that respect as they really are. These games (described starting on page 126) are traditionally "girls' games." No one told us we were doing batting practice when we played jacks or paddleball; they just gave us the jacks and encouraged us to use them. Boys can and should play jacks, too. Be sure not to limit their benefits to girls.

4. FLEXIBILITY Of the four components of fitness—endurance, strength, coordination, and flexibility—flexibility is quite probably the only one that your child has *no* chance of getting unless you help give it to him. This is true no matter how good his school program may be.

The Strange Rumor About Little-Boy Muscle and Little-Girl Muscle

When we were testing in Rye, Poughkeepsie, and Bethel, we ran into a lot of flexibility failures, particularly among the boys. Over and over again, from the kids and even from the coaches, we heard that boys' muscles are different from girls' muscles. This is the justification for a national problem in fitness, and it's totally untrue.

There are indeed three different kinds of muscle tissue in the body. There is skeletal muscle, which is the muscle that allows the skeleton to move, and which we exercise in this book. There is cardiac muscle, which is found in the heart. There is smooth muscle, which is contained within the walls of many body tubes, such as blood vessels and the digestive tract. *There is no little-boy muscle and no little-girl muscle.*

The difference between boys and girls, as far as their muscles are concerned, is the *thought* that there is a difference. Boys *think* they're stronger and less flexible than girls. Girls *think* they're weaker and more flexible than boys. They live up to those thoughts, and so those thoughts become reality. Most men don't do prolonged stretching exercises because they believe it's an exercise in futility, so they don't become flexible. We want to stress that. Boys aren't flexible because they don't do flexibility exercises, not because they are inherently inflexible.

All muscles do two things: contract and expand (get shorter and longer). If you want to build muscle bulk, you work on contraction, or strength, exercises. But if you don't want to get muscle-bound, you have to perform a flexibility exercise to lengthen the muscle again. A good weight-lifting program automatically combines a flexibility exercise in opposition to every strength exercise.

To create a good flexibility program within the context of building both strength and flexibility, think about the muscle that you are contracting. Then think about what you have to do to stretch that same muscle as far as it will go away from the contracted position without injury. (You'll see that we have built flexibility exercises directly into the program outlined in this book.)

One thing we absolutely know is that *if* girls aren't strong and boys aren't flexible (which is the usual pattern), they will probably develop back trouble as adults.

Another thing we absolutely know is that flexibility is the stepchild of most exercise programs in America. There are places to get good flexibility: modern dance and ballet classes, gymnastics, karate, professional- and semiprofessional-level sports programs with high-quality coaches. But most of the high-impact and low-impact videos and classes that we have screened do not have good flexibility components. Many coaches seem to believe that their male students are inflexible by nature, and coach accordingly.

If your child is participating in a particular sport, notice which body areas are most vulnerable to hyperextension and be sure to stretch those areas so that you can help your child avoid injury. This is one area where parents are going to have to get involved. (Note: be sure your child is warmed up before working through any flexibility program.)

3

How to Evaluate Your Child's Fitness

We think that the Kraus-Weber Minimum Muscular Fitness Test is a good place to start. It is a wellness predictor keyed to chronic low back pain, a major American health problem, and it's a minimum measurement of the major muscle systems.

What this test measures, which is not included in most other measurements, is flexibility. Results keep indicating that Americans are inflexible. We want that to change. So let's see how well you and your child do on Kraus-Weber; then we can move on from there. You can use the chart following the exercises to keep score.

KRAUS-WEBER MINIMUM MUSCULAR FITNESS TEST

ABDOMINALS WITH PSOAS*

Lie on your back with your legs straight and your hands clasped behind your neck. While someone holds down your feet, sit up once.

ABDOMINALS WITHOUT PSOAS

Lie on your back with your knees bent, your feet on the floor, and your hands clasped behind your neck. While someone holds down your feet, sit up once.

---

* The psoas muscle joins the front of the thigh to the small of the back. It allows you to lift your leg and is essential in holding your body in an upright posture.

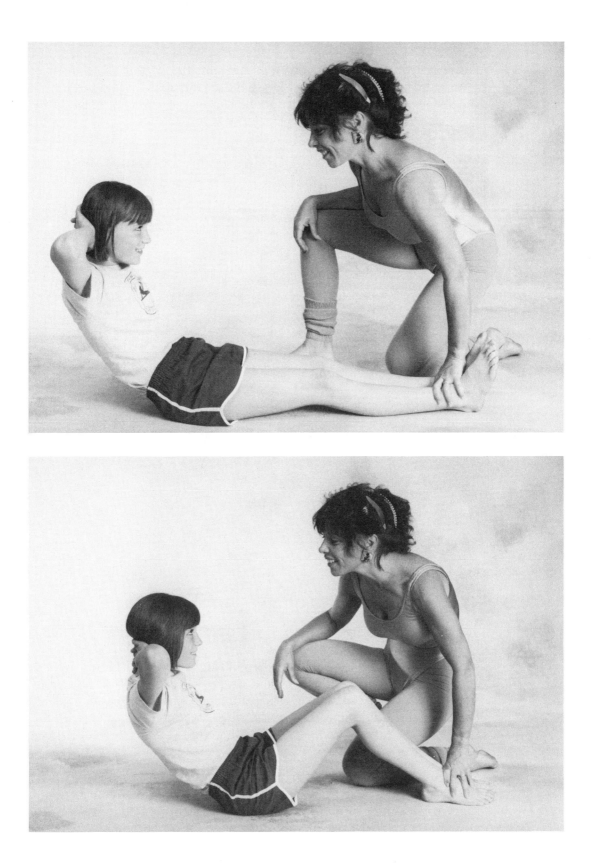

PSOAS

Lie on your back with your legs straight. Bend your arms and rest your hands, palms up, by your head. Raise your straight legs ten inches off the floor and hold for ten seconds.

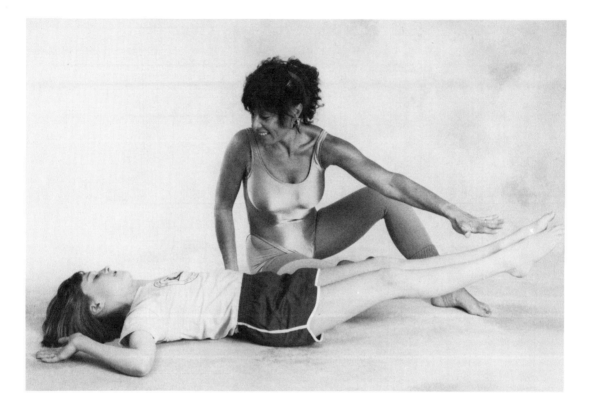

UPPER BACK

Lie on your stomach with your legs straight and your hands behind your neck and with a pillow placed under your hips. While someone holds down your legs, raise your head, chest, shoulders, and arms off the floor and hold for ten seconds.

LOWER BACK

Lie on your stomach with your legs straight and a pillow placed under your hips. Fold your arms in front of you and rest your head on your arms. While someone holds down your upper body, raise your straight legs at least ten inches off the floor and hold for ten seconds.

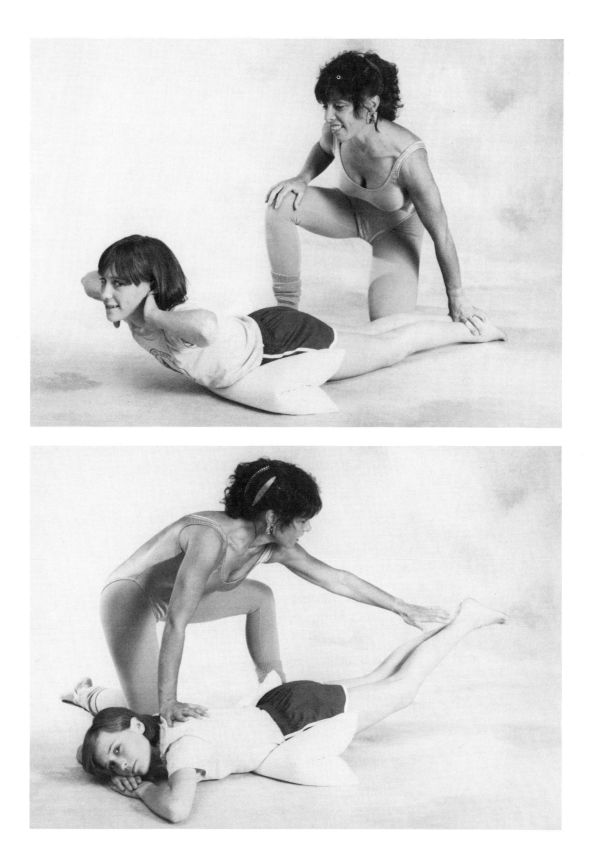

Flexibility

Stand with your feet together. Keeping your legs straight, slowly bend forward and touch the floor with your fingers. Hold for three seconds.

KRAUS—WEBER FITNESS TEST

	Pass	Fail How many
KW-1. Abdominals plus psoas One sit-up, legs straight		
KW-2. Abdominals minus psoas One sit-up, knees bent		
KW-3. Psoas Hold legs off floor, 10 secs.		
KW-4. Upper Back Hold upper body off floor, 10 secs.		
KW-5. Lower Back Hold straight legs off floor, 10 secs.		
KW-6. Flexibility Touch floor, straight legs, 3 secs.		

If your child failed KW-1 and KW-2, he has *weak abdominals.* He should do:

A-1	Sit-ups	Pages 34-35
A-2	Crossover Sit-ups	Page 44
A-5	Bicycle	Page 37
A-10	Lower Abdominal Lift	Page 40

If your child failed KW-3, he has *weak psoas muscles* and should do:

A-6	Up, Up, and Around	Page 38
B-5	Arch and Flatten	Page 47
B-6	Buttocks Up	Page 48
B-7	Back-Flat Leg Lower	Page 48
B-11	Cat and Horse	Page 50

If your child failed KW-4, he has a *weak upper back* and should do:

B-3	Prone Arm Lifts	Page 93
B-9	Paint the Wall	Page 92
B-16	Upper Body Lifts on Bench	Page 101

If your child failed KW-5, he has a *weak lower back* and should do:

B-2	Prone Leg Lifts	Page 46
B-10	Donkey Kick	Page 45
B-11	Cat and Horse	Page 50
B-17	Prone Leg Lifts on Bench	Page 100

If your child failed KW-6, he is *lacking in flexibility* and should do:

FL-1	Standing Forward Pulse with Straight Back	Page 60
FL-2	Standing Forward Pulse with Round Back	Page 51
FL-7	Sitting, Legs Straight, Forward Pulse	Page 41
FL-8	Feet-Apart Hamstring Stretch	Page 43
FL-9	Hamstring Psoas Stretch	Page 108

THE OPTIMUM TEST

After the Kraus-Weber Minimum Muscular Fitness Test we go on to the Optimum Test, which Bonnie developed many years ago. The Optimum Test is a well-rounded measurement that has the added benefit of measuring progress while, at the same time, serving as an exercise program in its own right.

The Optimum Test was designed to let children see how much they can do. It is not a test that measures passing and failing. Once one goal is reached, another is set. The Optimum Test encompasses measurements for the entire body, and unlike the Kraus-Weber Test, it is not limited to the areas pertaining only to the back.

Children love goals. The Optimum Test is your child's opportunity to set his own goals without competing with someone else. For example, the child who can do ten sit-ups can set his new goal to fifteen, then twenty. When he reaches twenty, he marks his success on his Optimum Test Chart and sets another new goal, possibly thirty. In this way he is continually striving to make himself better, while having a visual reminder of where he started.

The Optimum Test serves two purposes. One is to build regular habits of exercise into the child's day. The other is to measure progress so that the exercise is rewarding. The Optimum Test itself is a series of exercises and can either be done several times a week as part of your child's fitness program or simply be used as a periodic measurement of progress. It's fun to use the Optimum Test once every month so you and your child can see what has happened to his body. We know you'll both be pleased and slightly amazed at how quickly things get better.

OPTIMUM FITNESS TEST

OT-1. Bent-Knee Sit-ups (A)
Do A-1, page 34, performing as many sit-ups as you can in comfort. Do not "go for the burn." Write the number of sit-ups you did in the appropriate space on the Optimum Fitness Chart.

OT-2. Knee Bends (KB)
Do L-4, page 30. In the space provided on the chart, note how many slight, half, or full knee bends you can do.

OT-3. On-Knees Push-ups (KP)
If regular push-ups are too difficult, start with On-Knees Push-ups by doing B-12, page 90. Instead of making a box with your body, keep your back straight and lower your whole body to the floor, with weight resting on your hands and knees. Do as many On-Knees Push-ups as you can with your body straight from the shoulder to the knees. Record the number you did in the appropriate place on the chart.

OT-4. Pushups (P)
Now do SA-11, page 60, performing as many Push-ups as you can do with your body straight, and record that number in the appropriate place on the chart.

OT-5. Chin-ups (C)
Do SA-12, page 62, and mark how many Chin-ups you can do with palms facing forward. Repeat with palms facing backward.

The rest of the Optimum Fitness Test consists of special exercises you won't find elsewhere in the book. Start with:

OT-6. Upper Back (UB)

Lie on your stomach on the floor, with a pillow placed under your hips. Have someone hold down your feet, or tuck them under a chair or couch. Clasp your hands behind your neck and raise your head, chest, shoulders, and arms off the floor. Hold for five seconds, then lower. See how many times you can raise, hold, and lower your upper body and record that number in the space provided.

OT-7. Lower Back (LB)

Lie on your stomach on the floor, resting your head on your hands, and with a pillow placed under your hips. Have someone press down on your back. Straighten your legs and lift them as high as you can. Hold for five seconds, then lower. Raise, hold, and lower as many times as you can and record that number on the chart, noting how high you were able to raise your legs.

OT-8. Shoulder Flexibility (SF)

Grasp a three-quarter-inch, three-foot-long dowel at each end and hold it in front of you. Raise the dowel up and continue moving it over your head. Keep your arms straight, and stretch them as far back as you can without forcing. Record on the chart how far you were able to rotate your shoulders (eventually you will be able to move the dowel all the way behind you).

OT-9. Broad Jump (BJ)

Start in a stationary position with both feet together. Jump as far as you can with both feet together and record on the chart how far you were able to jump.

OT-10. Shuttle Run (SR)

Place two objects that will fit in your hand comfortably thirty feet away from you. Run back and forth from your starting point to the objects, picking up one object per trip and putting it on the starting line. (Place, don't throw, the objects on the starting line.) Record the time it took you to shuttle both objects from the thirty-foot line to the starting line.

OT-11. Hamstring Flexibility (HF)

Stand on a box or the lower step of a flight of stairs. Use a ruler to measure how far down your fingers can reach past the top of the box or stair, and record the number of inches above (if your fingers can't reach the lip of the box or stair) or below (if they pass the lip of the box or stair).

OT-12. Walking (W)

How far do you walk each day? How long does it take you? Measure a quarter of a mile from your house with the car odometer. Record in the space provided how many quarter miles you can walk in a day and how long it takes you to walk them.

OT-13. Jogging (J)

Jog at a slow, steady pace, slightly faster than a walk but slower than a trot. Jog the measured quarter mile you walked in OT-12. Record how many quarter miles you can jog in a day. (Note: If you experience any difficulty after jogging only a few steps, use the alternate jog-walk. Jog twenty steps, then walk twenty steps, and build from there. Soon you will be jogging all the way. Always be sure not to overdo it with jogging; don't push to the point of discomfort.)

THE OPTIMUM PROGRAM

The Optimum Fitness Test can become the Optimum Program. You can do it by itself, or in conjunction with your regular exercise program. Even if you don't use it as a program, it's a good idea to check yourself against it periodically to see how far you've come.

OPTIMUM FITNESS TEST GOALS AFTER EIGHT MONTHS

OT-1	Sit-ups (A)	30 in 1 minute
OT-2	Knee Bends (KB)	36 full, with flat feet
OT-3	On-Knees Push-ups (KP)	30 to 50
OT-4	Push-ups (P)	30 to 50
OT-5	Chin-ups (C)	30 to 50
OT-6	Upper Back (UB)	25 lifts
OT-7	Lower Back (LB)	25 lifts
OT-8	Shoulder Flexibility (SF)	Full rotation
OT-9	Broad Jump (BJ)	6 to 8 feet
OT-10	Shuttle Run (SR)	15 to 20 seconds
OT-11	Hamstring Flexibility (HF)	Touch palms to floor
OT-12	Walking (W)	5 miles
OT-13	Jogging (J)	3 miles

Do not start with your eight-month goals in the first three weeks, whether you're doing the Optimum Program or your regular exercise program. The value of both these programs is in building strength and flexibility into a *habit* of exercising. It's the habit that has the value. Build slowly and steadily and keep to the program.

Use this chart to indicate both your present state of fitness and your progress on the Optimum Fitness Test.

	Date	A	KB	KP	P	C	UB	LB	SF	BJ	SR	HF	W	J
Beg.			S											
			H											
			F											
4 wks.			S											
			H											
			F											
3 mos.			S											
			H											
			F											
6 mos.			S											
			H											
			F											
9 mos.			S											
			H											
			F											
1 yr.			S											
			H											
			F											
1+ yrs.			S											
			H											
			F											

4

How to Create a Fitness Program

Now that you know why you should have a fitness program for your child, and how to evaluate your child's progress, you are probably wondering what to do next. At the end of this chapter, you will find the exercises that will show you. These exercises are numbered to indicate which part of the body each emphasizes (see Appendix A, page 152). These exercises are also organized into programs that allow you to follow the instructions and illustrations one right after the other for a full body workout. With the exception of some flexibility and important back exercises, and the warm-up and cool-down that must be done at every exercise session, there are no repeated exercises. After you finish one exercise, turn the page and do the next.

FLEXIBILITY

You will notice we have not given flexibility exercises a special section. This is because it is important to do them often throughout your entire program while your muscles are warm. You will find flexibility exercises tucked in between all the other exercises. In order to avoid stiffness and soreness, knotting, and discomfort, it is important to mix in flexibility exercises this way.

The American Academy of Orthopaedic Surgeons (AAOS) calls for a minimum of one half hour of moderate exercise three times a week. That's for women and it's very much a minimum; we think the AAOS should reconsider that standard or let it be known that it's just a starting point for women who are out of shape. For our purposes, half an hour a day of general conditioning, flexibility, and low-impact aerobic exercises will prepare kids to do just about anything they want in sports within the limits of their natural ability.

Initially, we recommend that the child do two, four, or eight repetitions, as indicated. Starting with week three of the program, increase the number of repetitions by two. Every two or three weeks add two more. Stop adding repetitions before they become boring. Thereafter, begin working with weights. Be sure to cut the repetitions in half when you introduce the weights. See the weight program beginning on page 65.

All children between the ages of five and eleven should be able to do all the exercises in this book to some degree. Some will have an easy time, no matter the age at which they start, while others may feel and look awkward at the beginning. Both groups, the coordinated and the less coordinated, will improve.

The "natural athlete" may go on to competitive sports. The nonathletic type will become more athletic and enjoy his body more. Both groups will improve brain function. The most important thing to remember is to be consistent and patient. There is no timetable when it comes to strength, flexibility, and coordination. Improvement in every area comes with weekly repetition; this is the key.

Adults often have a daily exercise routine that doesn't vary significantly from day to day. Repeating the same routine every day doesn't work with children. Children lose interest quickly if they are doing only one program. The schedule on page 25 and the exercises in Program D (page 122), will enable you to create an excellent, varied program for your child—and for you too, if you choose to exercise along with him.

If your child plays a sport already, use the Sports Evaluation Chart on page 140. Take an afternoon and discuss how well he does with each sport. Identify the weak points and the strong ones. Be sure to stress the strong points so that your child does not feel criticized. As you progress in the fitness program, note the improvements in the sport. Be sure to point out these improvements continually to your child.

If your child's favorite sport is a season or two away, begin preparing for it early. Add exercises from the indicated areas in the sport-specific section (page 139) as a supplement to your daily exercise program. If the sport requires eye-hand coordination, be sure you begin working with the exercises in the eye-hand section early. Both you and your child will be amazed at the improvement over last year.

THE MUSIC INCENTIVE

You want to build an awareness in the child that he is about to begin something special, so before you begin your exercise program, prepare for it. The first step is to talk with your child and help him pick out music he wants to exercise to.

Music is one of the most important components of an exercise program. It is a driving force. It creates internal discipline. It sets a pace, slow or fast. Without music, exercise is a bore. With music, exercise can pass for dance and is a lot of fun. Make sure, when you are picking out the music, that it has a strong beat and that your child likes it. Each month you may both want to choose new music; variety not only keeps the exercises from getting boring, but also keeps the music from getting boring.

BUILDING EXERCISE HABITS

Exercise should become habitual. The more routine you can make it, the better the chance it will happen every day. Even storage space should be a matter of routine. Have a special place in the house where you exercise. Have a special place in the room for your weights and other exercise equipment. You can have your child change into exercise clothes, but if that's a hassle, don't let clothes undermine the program. Tack the schedule up on the wall where it's easy to see. Build in as many consistencies and habits around exercise as you can, so that it simply becomes part of the day, not something unusual.

Choose a time of day that is convenient, one that doesn't interfere with anything else you or your child would rather do, one that can be reserved every day as a rule, not as an exception. A particularly good time is the half hour to forty-five minutes just before homework time.

Choosing this time will accomplish two things. It will help release your child's tensions and eliminate the body toxins that have built up during the day. This will clear his mind so he can do the homework more easily, better, and in less time. Chances are your child has been sitting all through school, on the bus to and from school, and in front of the TV when he got home from school. Getting him up and active is a good idea before he has to sit down to do homework again. It may also be a way to break the momentum of television watching so that homework can begin.

Another good time for exercising is in a block of time between favorite TV shows. Be sure you choose a period of time that does not conflict with a preferred show. Making exercise part of a power play over a TV show defeats its purpose.

If your child exercises on his own, perhaps the half hour before dinner or while you are watching the evening news is best. And then again, first thing in the morning can be ideal for those children who are "morning people."

Some families set aside family exercise and music time. They simply get up forty-five minutes early. For this group, half an hour of sensible, vigorous exercise followed by fifteen minutes of sitting still and listening to music can set the tone of the whole day. Be creative, fit exercise into a period that works for you, but most of all, be consistent.

Schedule

Days one, three, and five

Always begin with the basic Warm-up (page 26).

Program A (page 34)	Abdominals, Lower Back, Midriff, and Arms
Program C-1 (page 65)	Weights, Resistance, and Coordination and Endurance
Program D (page 122) Choose from:	Gymnastics Equipment Eye-Hand Coordination Aerobics Sport-specific

Now end with the basic Cool-down (page 78).

Days two, four, and six

Don't forget the basic Warm-up (page 26)!

Program B (page 84)	Shoulders, Upper Back, Hips, and Legs
Program C-2 (page 107)	Weights, Resistance, and Coordination and Endurance
Program D (page 122) Choose from:	Gymnastics Equipment Eye-Hand Coordination Aerobics Sport-specific

Once, again, remember to cool down (see page 78).

Now that you have a schedule for the week, let's outline the basic Warm-up.

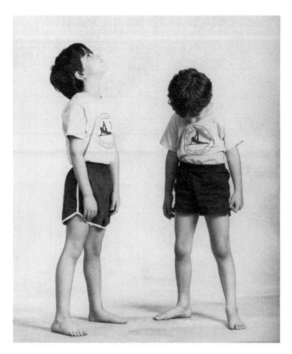

SA-7*   Head Tilt: Forward and Back
Stand with feet apart, hands resting at sides. Tighten abdominals and droop head forward. Keeping abdominals tight, arch head back as far as possible. Do two sets of eight repetitions.

* For complete listings of exercise numbers, see Appendixes A and B.

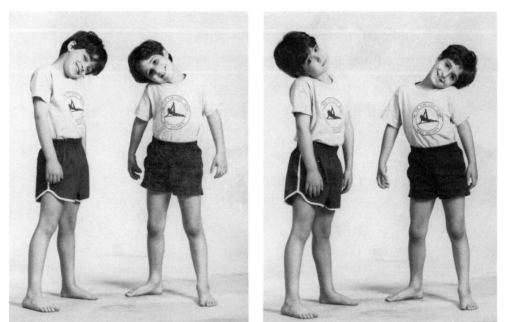

SA-8   Head Tilt: Side to Side
Stand with feet apart, hands resting at sides. Tighten abdominals and keep shoulders stationary. Droop right ear to right shoulder. Droop left ear to left shoulder. Do two sets of eight.

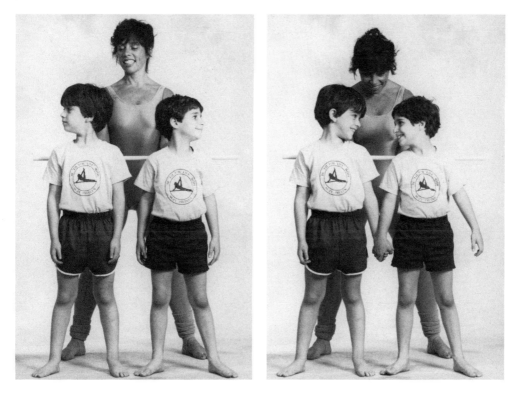

SA-9 Head Turn

Stand with feet apart, hands resting at sides. Tighten abdominals and keep shoulders stationary. Turn head to right as far as possible. Turn head to left as far as possible. Do two sets of eight.

SA-1 The Swim

a. *Center:* Stand with feet apart. Bend forward slightly from hips. Stretch right arm forward. Bend left elbow. Pull left arm back at shoulder height. Rotate arms forward in circles as if swimming. Elbows should bend on back pull and be fairly straight on the forward circle. Repeat eight times.

b. *Right:* Lean over right leg and rotate arms in same manner. Keep legs straight. Repeat eight times.

c. *Left:* Lean over left leg and make eight circles, keeping legs straight.

d. *Center:* Return to center for final set of eight.

SA-2 Arm Twist
Stand with feet apart. Place left hand on hip. Raise right arm to shoulder height. Bend arm slightly; palm should be facing up, elbow should be pointing down. Twist hand back as far as possible until palm faces up again (and beyond, if possible). Twist forward as far as possible until palm makes complete forward circle and faces up again. Be sure to keep arm bent. Repeat eight times. Change sides for eight more.

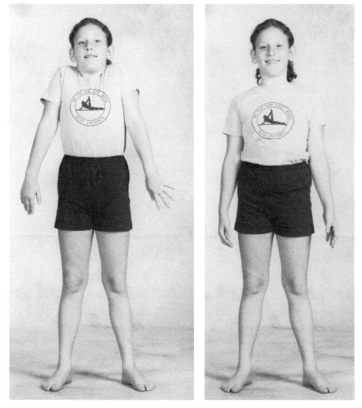

SA-3 Shoulder Shrugs
Stand with feet apart, arms resting at sides. Tighten abdominals. Raise shoulders up to ears and then lower them. Keep breathing. Do two sets of eight.

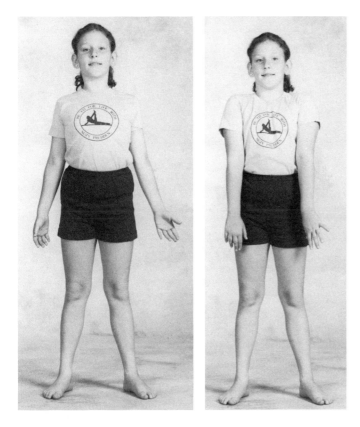

SA-4   Shoulders Back and Forth
Stand with feet apart, hands resting at sides. Round shoulders forward as if trying to touch them in front of body. Thrust shoulders back as if trying to touch them behind you. Do two sets of eight.

L-3   Side-to-Side Knee Bends
Stand with feet apart and arms outstretched sideways at shoulder height. Keep abdominals tight. Bend right knee, keeping left leg straight. Return to center. Bend left knee, keeping right leg straight. Do eight on each side.

L-4 Knee Bends
a. *Slight:* Stand with feet together, and stretch arms straight out in front at shoulder height. Keep abdominals tight, heels on floor. Bend your knees slightly. Stand straight again. Repeat eight times. Now stand with feet apart and repeat slight knee bends eight times.

b. *Half:* Stand as before, but this time bend knees halfway. Repeat eight times with feet together and eight times with feet apart.

c. *Full:* Stand as before. Bend knees until you are in a squatting position. Keep heels on floor if possible, but do not force them. Return to standing position. Repeat eight times with feet together and eight times with feet apart.

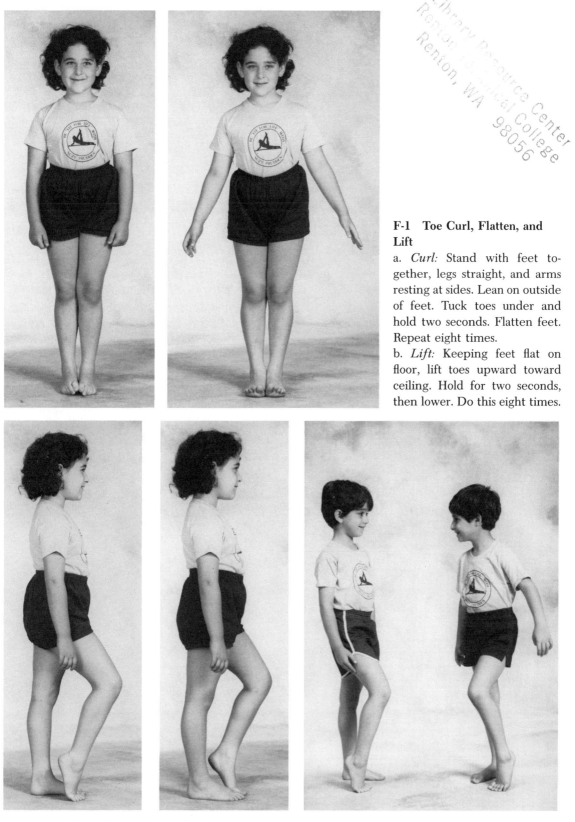

F-1 Toe Curl, Flatten, and Lift

a. *Curl:* Stand with feet together, legs straight, and arms resting at sides. Lean on outside of feet. Tuck toes under and hold two seconds. Flatten feet. Repeat eight times.

b. *Lift:* Keeping feet flat on floor, lift toes upward toward ceiling. Hold for two seconds, then lower. Do this eight times.

F-2 Alternate Heel Lift

Stand with feet together and arms resting at sides. Tighten abdominals and buttocks. Lift right heel off floor, resting on ball of right foot. Lower right heel and raise left heel simultaneously. Rest on ball of left foot. Repeat, alternating heel lifts, sixteen times, or two sets of eight.

F-3 Double Heel Lift

Stand with feet together, arms resting at sides. Tighten abdominals and buttocks. Slowly raise heels to stand on balls of feet. Hold four seconds. Slowly return to flat-footed position. Do this six times. (Most of the control is in the abdominal and buttock muscles.)

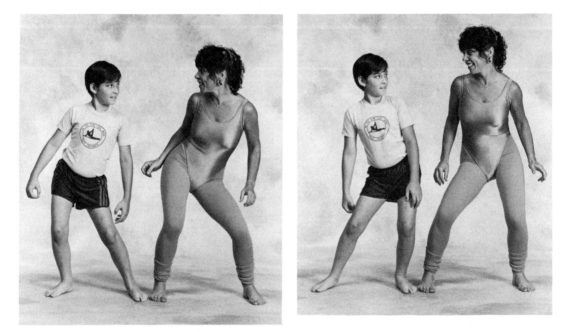

H-1 Bent-Knee Hip Wag

Stand with feet apart. Rest hands at sides and bend both knees slightly. Keeping both knees bent, push right hip out to right. Now push left hip out to left. Get a rhythm going, and repeat sixteen times, or two sets of eight.

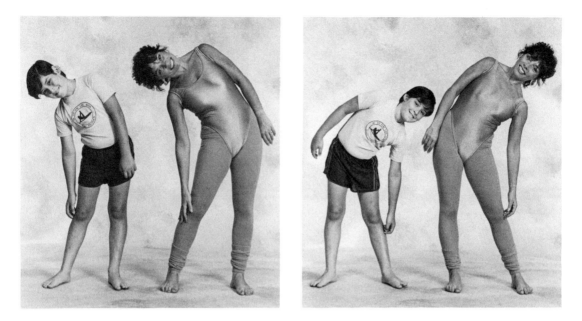

MB-4   Torso Tilt
Stand with feet apart. Rest hands at sides. Keeping legs straight, lean over to right. Slide right hand down right thigh. Stand straight. Lean over to left. Slide left hand down left thigh. Stand straight. Repeat eight times.

MB-5   Torso-Arm Swing
Stand with feet apart. Keep legs straight and abdominals tight. Raise arms and swing from side to side sixteen times, or two sets of eight.

PROGRAM A: DAYS ONE, THREE, AND FIVE

ABDOMINALS, LOWER BACK, MIDRIFF, AND ARMS

BEGIN WITH ABDOMINAL STRENGTH:

A-1 Sit-ups

Lie on back with knees bent and hands clasped behind neck. With someone holding down your feet, or with feet tucked under couch or chair. Tighten abdominals and slowly roll up to sitting position. Slowly roll down again. Repeat eight times.

If you cannot sit up with your hands clasped behind your neck, place your hands on your shoulders with the elbows forward, and roll up. Then place your hands behind your neck and roll down slowly to a count of six. If this is too difficult, place your hands across your chest and roll up. Again place your hands behind your neck and roll down slowly to the count of six. If it is still too difficult to sit up, use your hands to help you up any way you can. Roll down with your hands behind your neck to the count of six.

Find your own level of sit-up. Use the roll down to increase your ability.

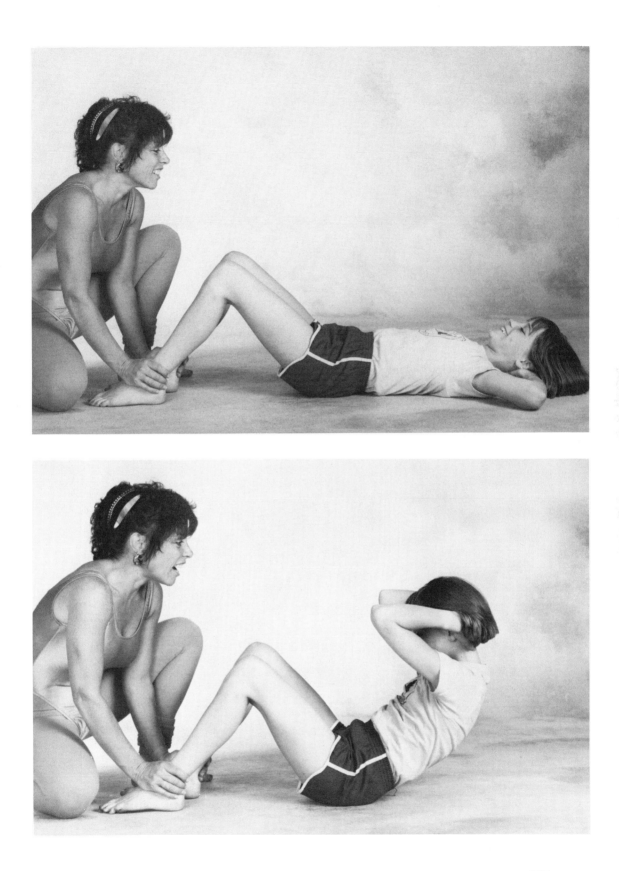

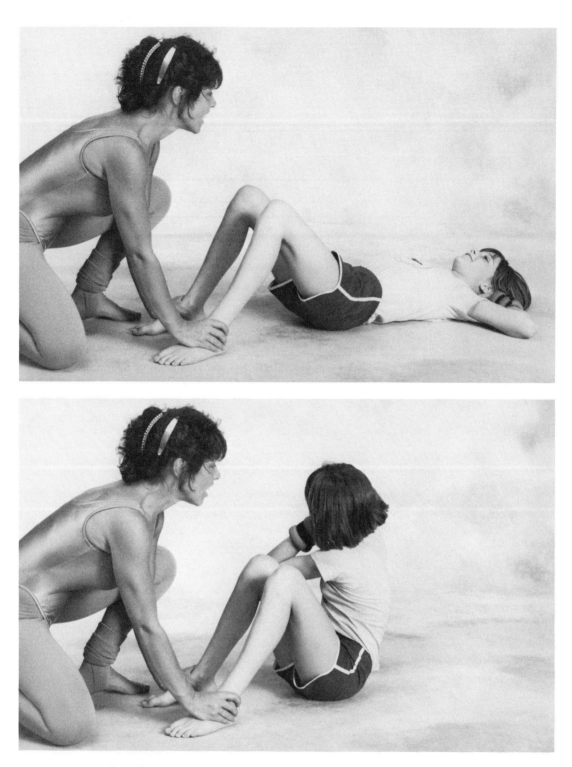

A-4 Sit-up to Alternate Elbow Touch

Lie on floor with knees bent, feet flat on floor, and hands clasped behind neck. Twist torso right and slowly sit up to place left elbow across right knee. Slowly roll down to starting position. Twist torso left and slowly sit up to place right elbow across left knee. Slowly roll down again. Repeat 8 times.

A-5 Bicycle

Lean back on elbows and forearms and stretch legs straight out in front of body. Raise right knee toward chest. While straightening right leg, and keeping it off floor, raise left knee toward chest. Repeat sixteen times, or for two sets of eight.

NOW ADD FLEXIBILITY:

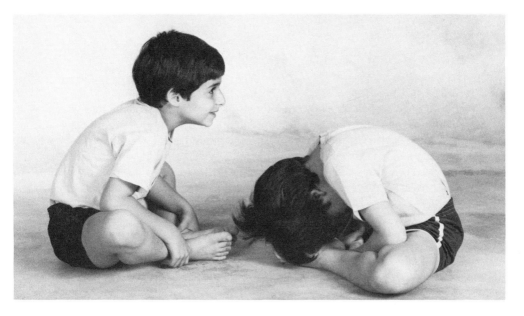

FL-5 Sitting, Feet Together, Forward Pulse

a. *Straight Back:* Sit on floor with knees bent. Soles of feet should be pressed together. Clasp ankles, keep back straight, and pulse* torso forward eight times.

b. *Round Back:* Now round back and pulse torso forward eight more times. Reach for toes with nose. Repeat sixteen times, or for two sets of eight.

* Because of concern about pulled muscles, the pulse has replaced the bounce. The pulse is a gentle pulling forward of the body in the direction you want to go and then releasing. To use the pulse effectively, try to pulse forward a little farther each time. Remember, the pulse does not force the muscles.

FL-6   Sitting, Feet Together, Knee Press
Sit as in FL-5, knees apart and soles of feet pressed together. Clasp ankles with hands and place elbows on knees. Use elbows to press knees toward floor. Release. Repeat eight times.

GO BACK TO MORE ABDOMINAL EXERCISES:

A-6   Up, Up, and Around
Lie on floor, resting on elbows and forearms; stretch legs straight out in front. Bend both knees and bring them up to chest. Straighten both legs so they are perpendicular to floor. Separate legs, circling them out and around, and lower them slowly, without bending knees, until they meet ten inches above floor. Hold position for two seconds and then bring knees to chest again. Repeat entire exercise four times. *(Important: If you experience any back pain, or lower back begins to arch, lower legs only halfway to floor. Work up slowly to ten-inch distance from floor.)*

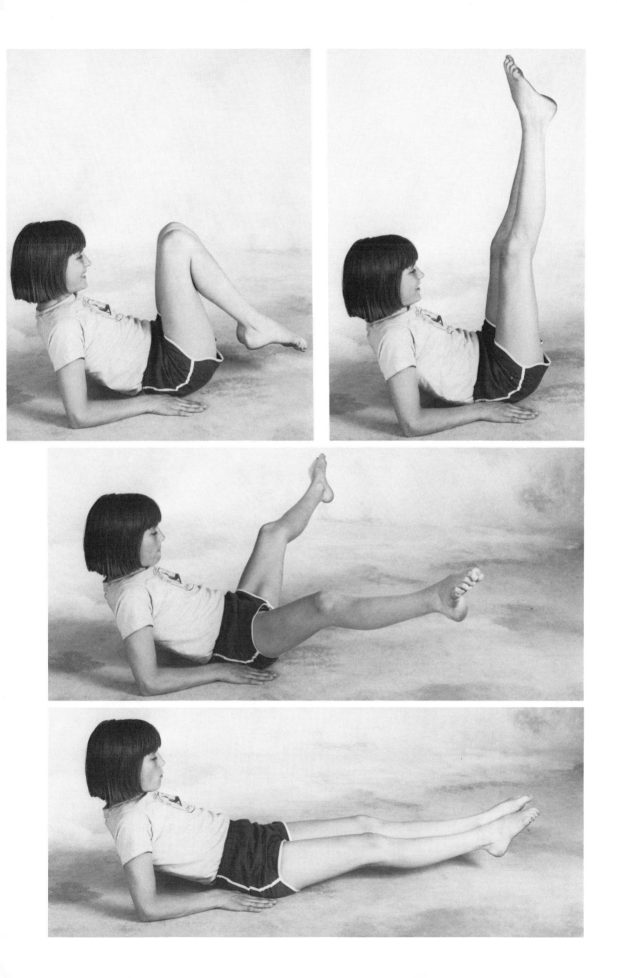

A-10   Lower Abdominal Lift

Lie on back with arms at sides, knees bent, and feet off floor. Tighten abdominals and bring knees toward chest, lifting buttocks off floor. Return to original position and repeat for two sets of eight.

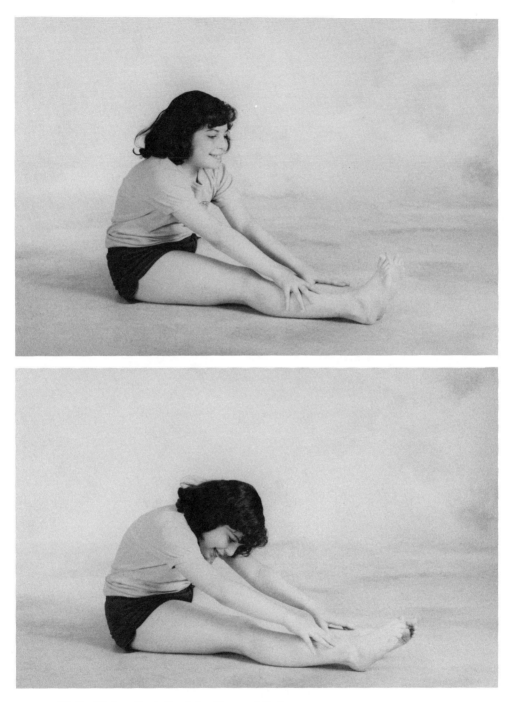

FL-7 Sitting, Legs Straight, Forward Pulse
a. *Straight Back:* Sit on floor with legs straight and together, knees facing ceiling. Clasp calves. Keeping back and legs straight, pulse torso forward eight times.
b. *Round Back:* Now round back. Keeping legs straight, pulse torso forward eight times. Repeat alternating series twice (do two sets).

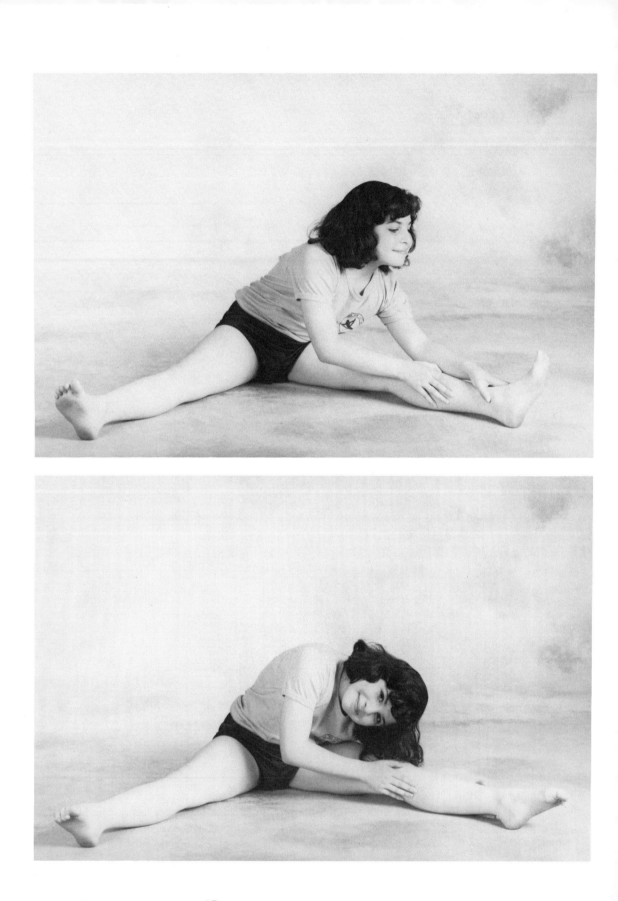

FL-8   Feet-Apart Hamstring Stretch

a. *Flexed:* Sit on floor with legs straight and apart. Knees should be facing ceiling. Flex feet. Clasp left leg with both hands and pulse torso forward as if trying to place chin on toes. Do this eight times. Change to right leg for eight more.

b. *Pointed:* Clasp left leg and point toes. Pulse over left leg as if trying to place left ear on left knee. Do this eight times, and change to right leg for eight more.

c. *Side Stretch:* Clasp left ankle with left hand. Raise hand and, stretching right arm as far as possible, pulse torso over left leg. Repeat eight times and change legs for eight more.

Repeat entire series (a, b, and c) once more.

RETURN TO MORE ABDOMINAL EXERCISES:

A-3 Hands Behind Neck, Knees to Elbows
Sit on floor with knees bent, feet flat on floor, and hands clasped behind neck. Lean back slightly and tighten abdominals, then bring torso forward while bringing knees up to touch elbows. Return feet to floor and lean back slightly again. Repeat sequence eight times.

A-2 Crossover Sit-ups
As in A-1 (page 34), lie on back with knees bent, feet resting on floor, and hands clasped behind neck. Have someone hold your feet down, or place feet under couch or chair. Roll into sitting position, crossing left elbow over right knee. Roll down to original supine (lying on your back) position to count of six. Roll into sitting position, crossing right elbow over left knee. Roll down to original supine position to count of six. As in A-1, find appropriate level and repeat eight times, always rolling down to a count of six.

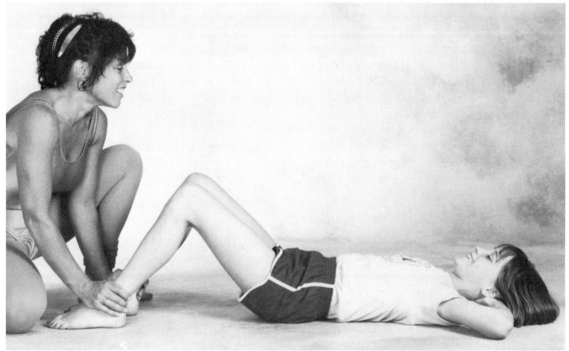

NOW MOVE ON TO LOWER BACK EXERCISES, INTERSPERSED WITH A FEW REMAINING ABDOMINAL EXERCISES:

B-10 Donkey Kick

Get on hands and knees. Keeping arms straight, pull right knee forward toward chest, lowering head at same time. Try to touch knee to nose while keeping arms straight. Then arch head up and, looking forward, kick leg out and straight up behind as far as possible. Repeat eight times with each leg.

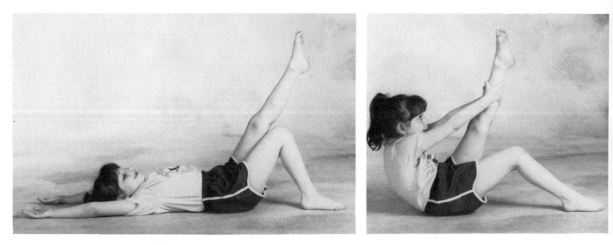

A-8 Ankle Catch

Lie on back with hands above head and legs straight. Raise straight left leg off floor as high as possible. Swing arms up, raising torso into sitting position, and clasp left ankle with both hands. Hold for three seconds and return to original position. Change legs and repeat. Perform entire sequence four times.

B-2 Prone Leg Lifts

Lie on stomach with legs outstretched. Rest head on folded arms. Keeping buttocks and abdominals tight, and hips on floor, raise and lower right leg. Now raise and lower left leg. Repeat alternate leg lifts eight times each leg.

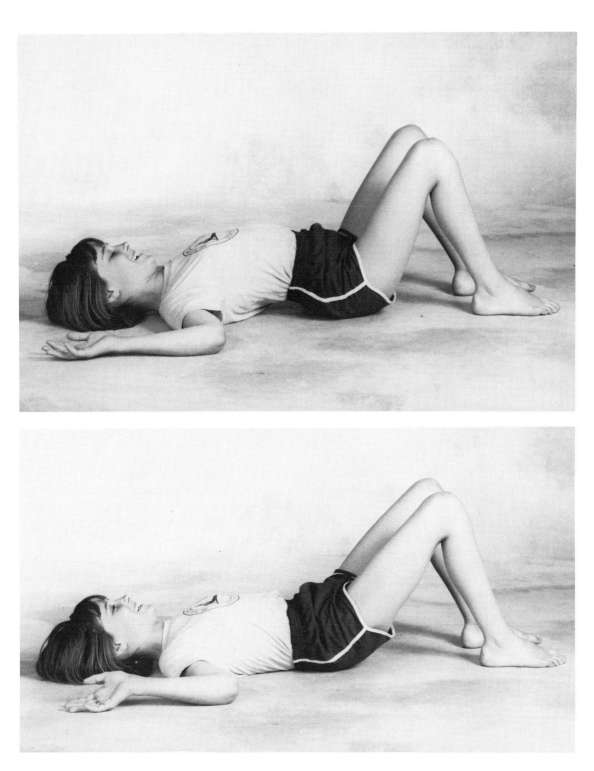

B-5 Arch and Flatten
Lie on back with knees bent and feet on floor. Bend elbows, resting hands by head.
Keeping buttocks and upper back on floor, arch lower back. Now press lower back
against floor and hold four seconds. Repeat arch-and-flatten sequence eight times.

B-6   Buttocks Up

Lie on back as in B-5 (last page). Tighten buttocks and abdominals. Lift buttocks off floor as high as possible and hold four seconds. Now lower buttocks to floor to count of eight. Repeat four times.

B-7   Back-Flat Leg Lower

Lie on back, legs outstretched, elbows bent, hands resting by head. Pull knees in toward chest. Now straighten legs up, perpendicular to floor, and hold two seconds. Slowly lower legs as far as possible, keeping back flat on floor. *(Important: If the small of your back arches off the floor, you've gone too far. Go back to a point at which it does not want to arch off the floor, and use that as lowest point.)* Hold legs straight out at lowest point for four seconds. Then bend knees over chest again. Repeat eight times.

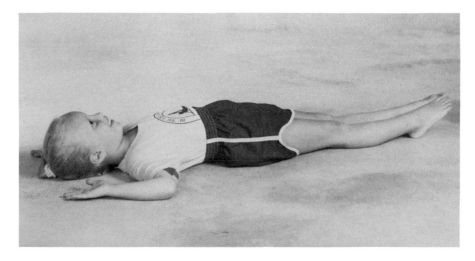

B-11 Cat and Horse

Get on hands and knees, pull in adominals, drop head, and round back upward as if making a cat back. Hold two seconds, then release abdominals, lift head, and arch back downward, making it sway. Hold two seconds. Repeat eight times.

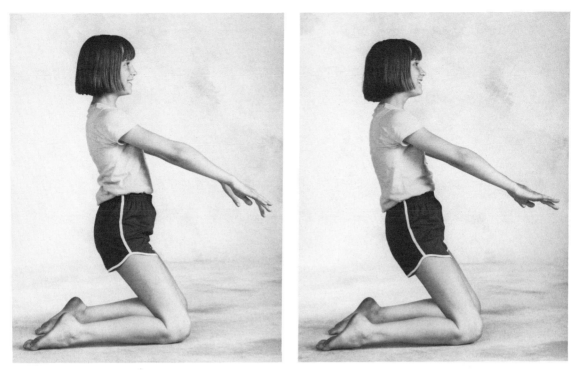

B-8   Kneeling Pelvic Tilt

Get on knees with hands stretched out at a 45-degree angle in front of body. Keeping upper back straight, arch lower back, thrusting buttocks backward. Then tighten abdominals and tuck buttocks under. Thrust outward and tuck under eight times.

ONCE MORE, BRING IN FLEXIBILITY:

FL-2   Standing Forward Pulse with Round Back

Stand with feet apart. Rest hands at sides and keep legs straight. Drop torso forward (touch hands to floor if possible). Pulse hands toward floor eight times. Now pulse over right leg eight times. Pulse over left leg eight times. Return to center and pulse eight more times.

FL-3 Standing Alternate Toe Touch
Stand with feet apart. Stretch arms out to the sides at shoulder height and keep legs straight. Bend forward and touch right foot with left hand, keeping right hand raised in air. Now touch left foot with right hand, keeping left hand raised in air. Get a rhythm going and alternate back and forth for two sets of eight.

MOVE ON TO THE MIDRIFF:

MB-1 The Tree
Stand with feet apart. Raise arms above head, slightly bent, palms facing inward. Bend right knee and lean torso to right. While straightening right leg, bend left knee and swing arms and torso over left leg. Repeat for two sets of eight.

MB-7 Forward Bend, Torso-Arm Swing
Stand with feet apart, resting hands at sides. Bend torso forward from hips. Raise right arm up and twist torso to right, following movement with head and left arm. Now twist torso to left and raise left arm, following movement with head and right arm. Swing arms and torso back and forth for two sets of eight.

MB-3 Leaning Overhead Arm Stretch

Stand with feet apart, resting hands at sides. Rest left hand on left thigh and raise right hand above head. Lean torso to left and bounce four times. Change sides and repeat. Do series twice.

MB-2 Dowel Arm Swing

Stand with feet apart. With both hands, grasp a three-quarter-inch, three-foot-long dowel at each end. Keeping legs straight, swing arms from side to side for sixteen times, or two sets of eight.

NOW MOVE ON TO ARM EXERCISES, WITH SOME ABDOMINAL, FOOT, AND FLEXIBILITY EXERCISES INTERSPERSED.

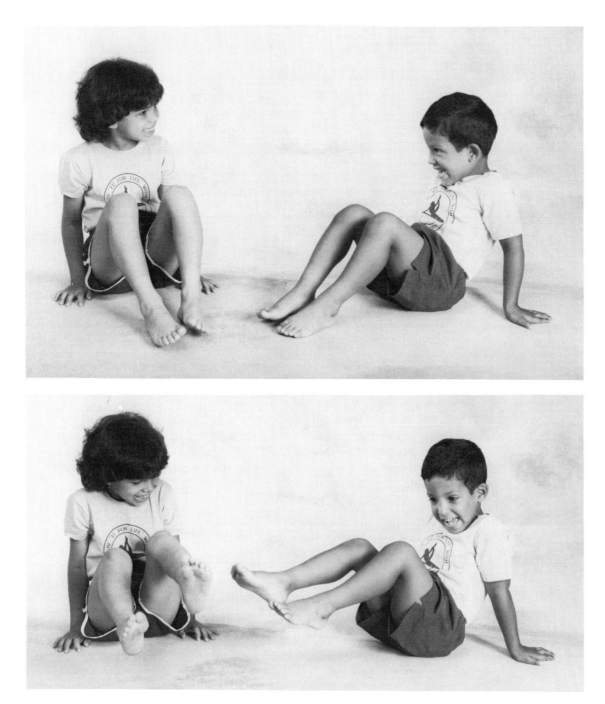

A-7 Sitting Foot Bounce
Sit on floor with feet flat, knees bent, and hands resting on floor behind body. Bounce feet up and down, raising knees toward chest and touching feet to floor, for two sets of eight.

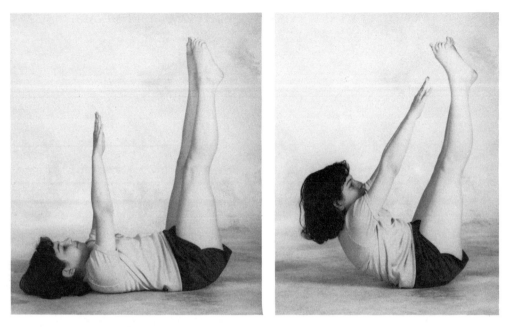

A-9 Body Folds

Lie flat on back with arms and legs stretched up so that body forms a U. Feet should be pointed. Tighten abdominals. In one motion, lift torso off floor, reaching for feet. Return to original position. Repeat eight times.

SA-14 Push a Pebble with Your Nose

Get down on hands and knees. Sit back, almost on heels, with arms stretched out in front as far as possible. Place weight on arms, bend elbows, and begin to pull head and torso forward, keeping chest close to floor. When you have gone as far as you can, straighten arms and lift head and chest up, while dropping buttocks. Return to starting position and repeat six times.

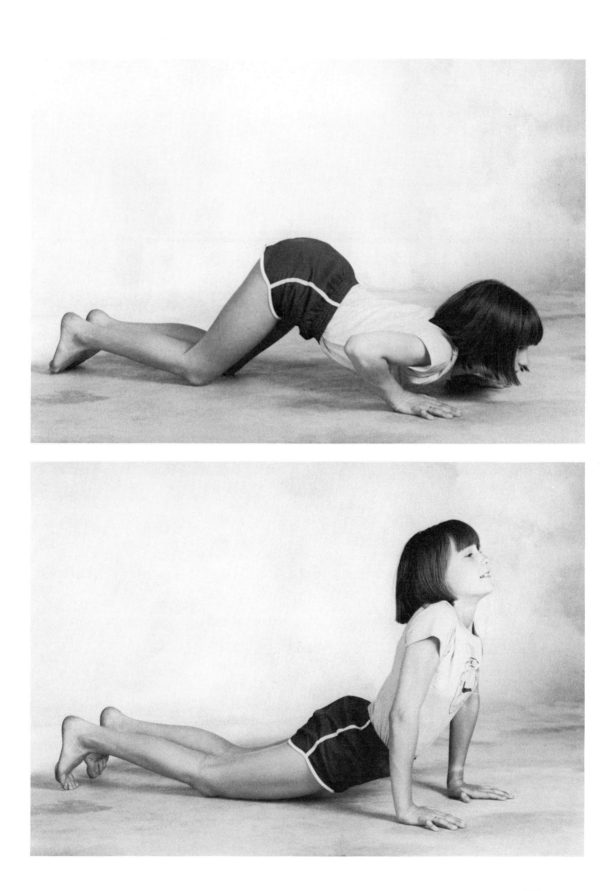

SA-15 Arm Twist, Back-Hand Touch, Palm-up Stretch
Stand with feet apart. With palms up, stretch arms straight out to sides. Twist palms downward and around until hands are upside down. Bring straight arms together to meet in front of body (backs of hands should touch). Now twist hands upward until palms face ceiling again. Stretch straight arms back as far as comfortable. Get a rhythm going and repeat eight times.

SA-5 The Backstroke
Stand with feet slightly apart, hands resting at sides. Bend right arm and raise it, touching back of hand to cheek with elbow thrust back. Straighten arm up, then back, and circle it backward until it rests at side again. Change arms and repeat entire sequence eight times.

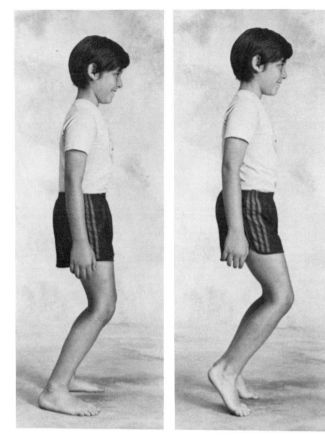

F-6 Knee Wag

Stand with feet together. Rest hands at sides and bend knees slightly. Tighten abdominals and tuck buttocks under. Keeping centered, allow ankles to bend right, thrust knees to right. Then allow ankles to bend left, thrust knees to left. Get a rhythm going, and do two sets of eight knee wags in each direction.

F-7 Bent-Knee Heel Lift

Stand with feet together. Rest hands at sides and bend knees slightly. Pretend there's a low ceiling above your head, so you cannot lift upper body upward. Keeping knees bent, lift both heels off floor. (All action should take place in legs.) Hold for two seconds. Keeping knees bent, return heels to floor. Repeat heel lift eight times.

SA-11 Push-ups

Lie on stomach. Rest with legs apart, toes and top of balls of feet on floor. Place hands on floor next to shoulders, palms down. Keeping body absolutely straight, push against floor until arms are straight and body is raised. Keep body straight and lower it to floor. (Be sure not to raise buttocks too high or drop tummy too low.) Start with two and work up to twelve.

If you cannot perform a push-up, get into the raised push-up position any way you can and then, keeping body absolutely straight, lower body slowly to count of eight. Repeat four times.

FL-1 Standing Forward Pulse with Straight Back

Stand with feet apart and hands clasped behind buttocks. Keeping legs and back straight, pulse torso forward eight times. Now pulse torso forward over straight right leg eight times. (Remember to keep back straight.) Pulse torso forward over straight left leg eight times. Then return to center and pulse eight more times.

FL-17 Side Knee Bend, Straight-Leg Stretch

Stand with feet apart, hands resting at sides. Bend over left leg. Now bend left knee and lower hands to floor. Keeping hands as close to floor as possible (eventually *on* floor), straighten left leg. Repeat bend-and-straighten motion four times, and then change sides for four more.

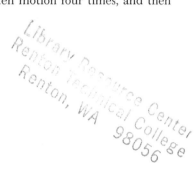

SA-10 Hand Walk-Forward Droop

Stand with feet apart, hands at sides. Tighten abdominals and keep legs straight. Bend forward at hips and place right hand on floor. Place left hand on floor farther out and, keeping feet in place, walk forward on hands three steps. Now, keeping arms and legs straight, droop stomach toward floor. Then raise buttocks in air and walk hands back again. Stand straight, put hands on hips. Repeat six times.

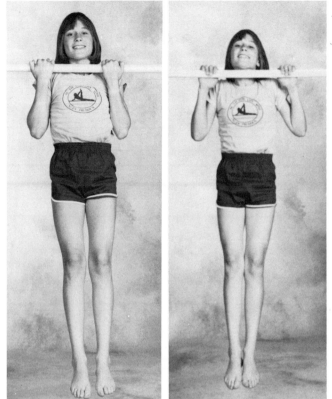

SA-12 Chin-ups

a. *Palms Inward:* Stand beneath chinning bar. Grasp it in both hands with *palms turned inward.* Pull body up until chin is over bar. Now slowly lower body. Start with one chin-up and work up to twelve.

b. *Palms Outward:* Stand beneath chinning bar. Grasp in both hands with *palms turned outward.* Pull body up until chin is over bar, then slowly lower body. Start with one and work up to twelve.

c. *Let-downs:* If you cannot do one chin-up, stand on a chair that is placed slightly behind and out of the way of your legs when they are lowered. Grasp chinning bar in both hands with palms turned inward so that chin is over bar. Lift feet off chair and slowly lower body to count of eight until arms are straight. Do let-downs five times, rest, then do five more with palms turned outward.

SA-13 Chin-up Knee Lifts

Get into raised chin-up position with palms turned inward. Raise knees to chest and then lower them. Repeat for a total of eight times.

FINISH THE CONDITIONING PROGRAM WITH FLEXIBILITY EXERCISES
THAT COMBINE EQUIPMENT AND COORDINATION:

E-3   Frisbee Alternate Toe Touch
Hold a Frisbee in each hand. Stand with feet apart, arms stretched out to the sides at
shoulder height. Tighten abdominals and keep legs straight. Touch right foot with left
Frisbee, raising right arm in air. Then touch left foot with right Frisbee, raising left
arm in air. Get a rhythm going and alternate for two sets of eight.

E-6   Frisbee Alternate Bent-Knee Toe Touch and Reach
(This exercise has four movements. We have divided it into two parts to make it easier
to understand.)
a. *Toe Touch:* Stand with feet apart and hold a Frisbee in each hand. Bend left leg and
reach down to touch left foot with Frisbee held in right hand; raise left Frisbee into air
behind body. Now straighten left leg, bend right knee, and lower left Frisbee to touch
right foot; raise right Frisbee behind body.
b. *Reach:* Stand straight and raise right Frisbee in air to left. (Right arm should cross in
front while left arm is stretched behind body at 45-degree angle.) Bring right Frisbee
back to right side and lower it behind body at 45-degree angle. Raise left Frisbee
above head and to right. It should cross in front of body. Get a rhythm going (touch
left, touch right, reach left, reach right) and repeat four times.

PROGRAM C-1: DAYS ONE, THREE, AND FIVE

WEIGHTS, RESISTANCE, AND COORDINATION AND ENDURANCE

Now begin Program C-1 with weight exercises, move on to resistance exercises, and finish up with coordination and endurance exercises. Be sure not to skip the flexibility exercises interspersed among the others, even though you may have done them in Program A, in the first half of this workout.

W-1 Sawing Wood
Strap one-pound weights around wrists or hold one-pound dumbbell in right hand. Rest left hand and knee on bench and allow weighted right arm to hang down. Bend right elbow and raise it in straight line as high up behind body as possible. Lower and straighten arm to original position. Repeat eight times. Transfer dumbbell, if you are using it, to left hand, and repeat exercise eight times on left side.

W-2 Shoulder Shrug
Strap one- or two-pound weights around wrists, or hold one- or two-pound weights in each hand. Allow arms to rest at sides, and place feet slightly apart. Keeping abdominals tight, raise and lower shoulders for two sets of eight.

W-3 Biceps Curl
Hold one- or two-pound weights in each hand with palms facing forward and arms resting at sides. Stand with legs straight and feet slightly apart. Tighten abdominals and bend right arm, bringing right hand to right shoulder (palm should face shoulder). While lowering right hand, bring left hand to left shoulder. Repeat whole exercise (right and then left hand up) for a total of sixteen times.

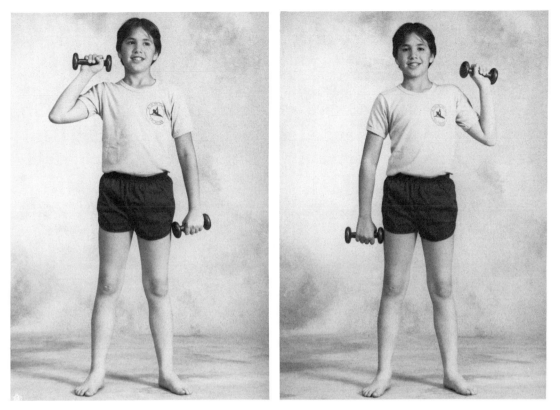

W-4   Reversed Curl

Hold one- or two-pound weights in both hands, palms facing back and arms resting at sides. Stand with legs straight and feet slightly apart. Bend right arm and raise right hand to right shoulder, palm facing out. Lower right hand and raise left hand to left shoulder, palm facing out. Repeat whole exercise (alternating right and then left hand up) for a total of sixteen times.

FOR FLEXIBILITY, DO ANOTHER **Standing Forward Pulse with Straight Back** (FL-1, PAGE 60). THEN CONTINUE WITH:

W-5   Butterflies

Hold one- or two-pound weights in both hands, with arms resting at sides. Stand with feet slightly apart. With palms facing inward, raise straight arms outward to meet above head. Now lower arms to sides. Repeat four to eight times.

67

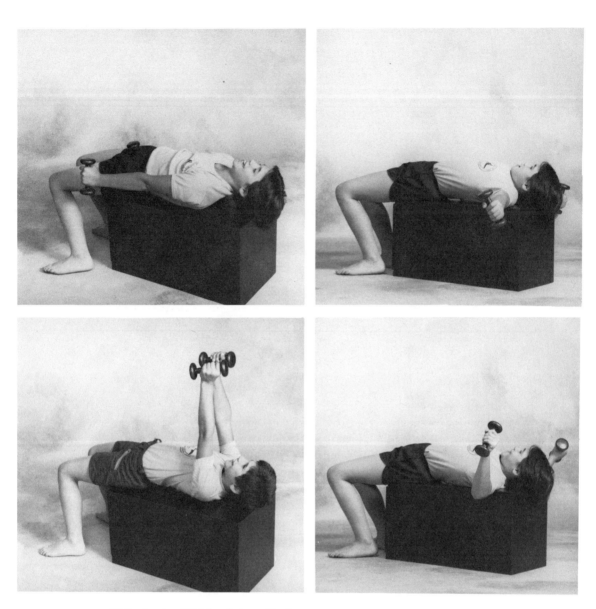

W-8 Supine Weighted Arm Circle

Lie on back on bench. Feet should rest on floor. With one- or two-pound weights in both hands, hold arms straight at sides. Keeping them straight, raise them out at sides to shoulder level. Now lift them straight up above chest. Hold for two seconds. Bend elbows, lowering arms down to sides again. Return to straight-arm starting position. Repeat six times.

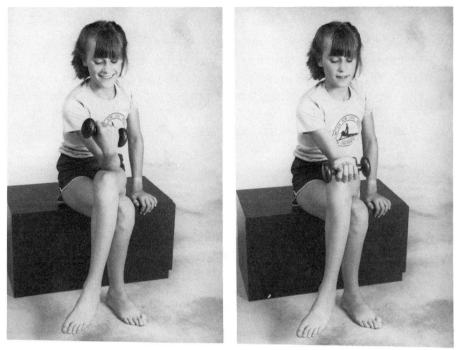

W-10 Wrist Curl

Sit on chair or bench. Cross left leg over right. Hold one- or two-pound weight in right hand and rest right elbow on left thigh. With palm facing up and arm held still, bend wrist back and down, then forward and up. Repeat eight times with each hand.

W-13 Seated Dumbbell Press

Sit on bench or chair. Hold one- or two-pound weights with both hands. Raise arms straight above head. Lower hands behind neck, pointing elbows outward. Straighten arms up again. Lower and raise hands eight times.

FOR MORE FLEXIBILITY, DO **Feet-Apart Hamstring Stretch** (FL-8, PAGE 43).

RESISTANCE

Resistance exercises are important for further muscle development. For the following exercises you can use a rubber strap, a rubber band, a slice of rubber tubing from an inner tube, or five-eighths-inch hospital tubing, as shown here. Cut the strap or tubing about three feet in length.

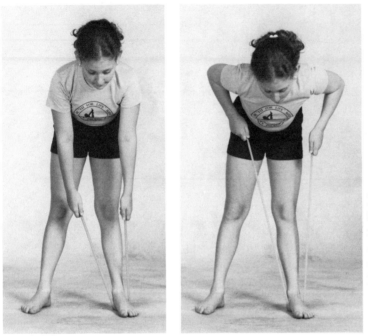

R-1 Tube Pull
Stand with feet apart. Hold tubing at either end. Bend forward and place center of tubing under left foot. Tubing will be relaxed. Keep body bent forward and stationary. Raise and lower elbows to tighten tubing. Do one or two sets of eight.

R-2 Tube Chest Stretch
Stand with feet apart. Hold tubing at shoulder height in front of body. Tube should be tight but not taut. Keeping abdominals tight and back straight, stretch arms out to sides while stretching tube. Slowly return to starting position. Repeat twelve times.

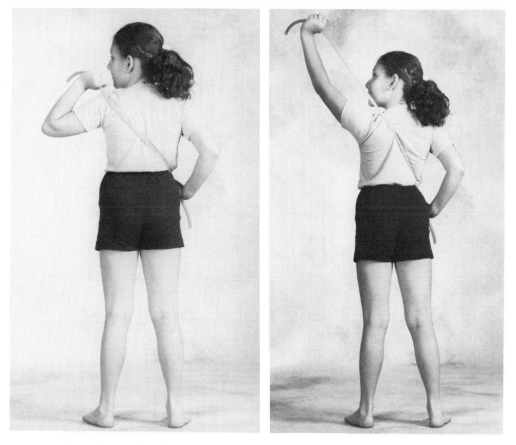

R-3 Tube Back and Arm Stretch
Stand with feet apart. Hold tubing behind back. Place right hand on hip, left hand by left shoulder. Holding right hand still, raise and lower left hand as far as possible. Repeat twelve times. Change sides and repeat twelve times.

NOW PERFORM **Standing Forward Pulse with Round Back** (FL-2, PAGE 51).

COORDINATION AND ENDURANCE

CE-1 Walking
Tighten abdominals and straighten back. Walk across room or yard, as shown here. Mark off your neighborhood into quarter-mile segments. Walk several miles a day in quarter-mile increments. Be sure to pick up the speed of your walk and maintain that speed all the time you are walking. Walking ten to fifteen miles per week is today's most popular low-impact aerobic exercise.

CE-2   Pigeon and Upright Duck Walk
a. *Pigeon:* Tighten abdominals and hold back straight. Turn feet inward and walk across room or yard.
b. *Duck:* Tighten abdominals and hold back straight. Turn feet out and walk across room or yard.

CE-5   Squatting Duck Walk
With feet apart, squat down as low as possible. Walk across floor or yard in this position. (Try quacking as you go!)

HERE'S A NEW FLEXIBILITY EXERCISE:

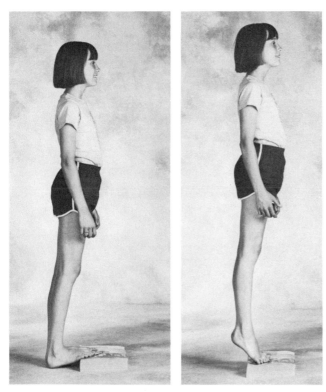

FL-15   Achilles Tendon Stretch

Place large book on floor. Stand on book with front half of foot. Allow heels to rest on floor for five seconds. (Do not bounce heels down.) Raise heels. Rest on ball of foot for two seconds. (This exercise is much easier to do with tightened buttock and abdominal muscles.) Repeat entire exercise eight times.

NOW BACK TO COORDINATION AND ENDURANCE:

CE-11   Jumping Jacks

Jump, landing with feet apart and arms outstretched at a 45-degree angle above shoulders. Jump, landing with feet together and hands at sides. Keep abdominals tight. Do two sets of eight.

CE-12 Skip

a. *Forward:* Step on right foot. Hold left foot up and hop on right foot. Step on left foot. Hold right foot up and hop on left foot. Get a step-hop, step-hop rhythm going, and cross floor or yard.

b. *Backward:* Step back on left foot. Hold right foot up in front. Hop backward once on left foot. Step back on right foot. Hold left foot up in front. Hop backward once on right foot. Get a step-hop, step-hop rhythm going, and cross floor or yard.

CE-6 Pony Bucks

Get on hands and feet. Bend knees and keep buttocks up. Kick feet up, keeping them close to buttocks. Do one or two sets of eight.

74

CE-14 Monkey Walk

Get on hands and feet. Straighten legs and keep backside up. Walk back and forth or around the room twice.

CE-15 Wheelbarrow

With both legs held in air by parent or friend, rest weight on both hands. *Important: Be sure back does not sway. If back sags, have parent or friend grasp legs closer to body.* Walk on hands back forth or around the room twice.

E-1 Jump Rope

This is the simplest, least expensive, most effective piece of equipment available! Try some of these variations. It is not necessary to do all variations every day. Pick and choose. Start with thirty jumps and work up to two to three minutes of jumping.

a. *Plain and Simple:* Hold jump rope in both hands, one hand at each end of rope. Rest rope on floor behind body. Swing rope up over head. As it lands on floor, jump over it. Get rhythm going and build up to 100 jumps without stopping.

b. *Reverse Plain and Simple:* Rest rope on floor in front of body. Swing it up over head. As it lands on floor behind body, jump over it. Build up to 100 jumps without stopping.

c. *Big Jump, Little Jump:* Rest rope on floor behind body. Swing it up and over head. As it lands on floor in front, jump over it. Swing rope up over head again. As it reaches highest point above head, make a very small jump, and when it lands on floor, make a big jump over it. Get a rhythm going and build up to 100 big jumps without stopping.

d. *Jump, Hop Right—Jump, Hop Left:* Place rope behind body. Swing it up over head. When it reaches floor in front, jump over it. Again, swing rope over head. When it reaches its highest point above head, hop on right foot. Let rope swing down in front. Jump over it with both feet. When it swings over head again, hop on left foot. Continue. Build up to 100 jumps without stopping. Practice the jump-hop series in reverse, starting with rope in front of body. Build up to 100 hop/jumps.

e. *Forward Step, Step Left—Forward Step, Step Right:* (This is a good pattern for someone who is having difficulty jumping with two feet.) Place rope behind body. Swing it over head. When it reaches ground in front, step over it with right foot. Keep rope swinging over head. When it reaches topmost arc over head, step on left foot. Step with right foot again when rope touches floor. Right foot is always the foot going over the rope. Build up to 100 steps without stopping. After 25, change to left foot going over rope, and right foot stepping between. When stepping becomes easy, jump onto right foot instead of stepping. Then practice jumping in reverse, starting with rope in front of body. Build up to 100 repetitions.

f. *Running Across Room or Yard:* Place rope behind body. Swing it up over head. As it reaches the ground, move forward and run over it. Lead with right foot for 50 steps. Lead with left foot for 50 steps. Reverse process and run backward. Lead with right foot for 50 steps. Lead with left foot for 50 steps.

g. *Double-Time Run:* Place rope behind body. Swing it up and over head double time. Every time rope reaches floor in front, step over it with running or prancing motion. Run in place for 100 jumps. Then reverse and run backward for 100 jumps.

h. *Jump Squatting:* Shorten rope in both hands. Squat with rope behind body. Bring rope up over head. When it reaches floor in front, jump over it. Maintain squat position and jump rope. Build up to 100 jumps. Reverse. Again build up to 100 jumps.

NOW ANOTHER FLEXIBILITY EXERCISE:

FL-18 Feet Apart, Bottoms Up, and Chest Stretch
Stand with feet apart. Rest hands at sides. Bend forward from hips and, keeping legs straight, walk hands out on floor to form a wide upside-down V with body. Keep knees straight and stretch torso back and forward. Repeat rocking eight times.

DO ANOTHER **Frisbee Alternate Toe Touch** (E-3, PAGE 63), THEN TRY:

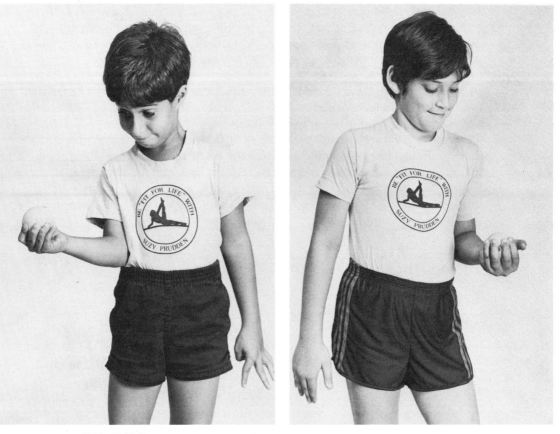

E-7 Ball Squeeze
Sit or stand and hold rubber ball in one hand. Squeeze ball as hard as possible. Keep breathing and hold for four seconds. Release for four seconds. Repeat four to eight times, change hands, and repeat four to eight times.

FINALLY, DO ONE MORE FLEXIBILITY EXERCISE: **Sitting, Legs Straight, Forward Pulse** (FL-7, PAGE 41).

Now is the time to add the activities outlined in Program D (page 122). We've given them a special section of their own to allow you to choose those most beneficial to your needs.

COOL-DOWN

Once you've finished the workout for the day, always end the daily program with a cool-down, using exercises you've already learned:

MB-1	The Tree	page 52
SA-3	Shoulder Shrugs	page 28
SA-4	Shoulders Back and Forth	page 29

IN ADDITION TO THESE, DO THE FOLLOWING EXERCISES FOR THE FEET:

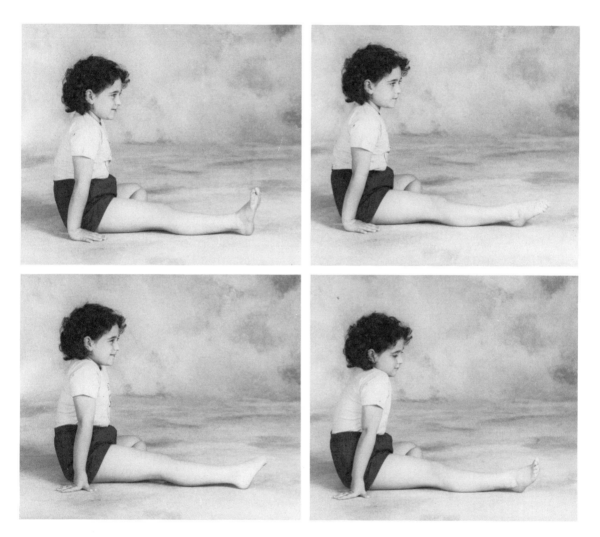

F-4 Foot Works

a. *Flex and Point:* Sit on floor with right leg stretched out and left leg bent comfortably in front. Rest arms at sides with hands on floor. Keep right leg straight with knee facing ceiling. Flex foot toward face and hold for two seconds. Now point foot and hold two seconds, then relax foot.

b. *In and Out:* Making sure knee is still facing ceiling, twist foot inward and hold two seconds. Twist foot outward and hold two seconds.

Repeat whole sequence four times, change legs, and repeat four more times.

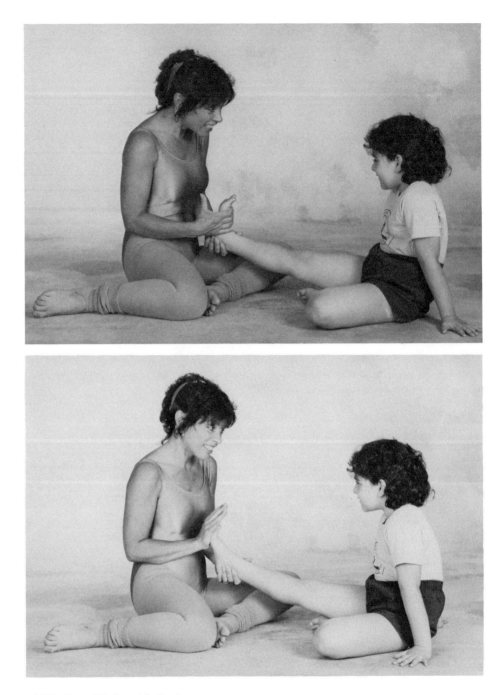

F-5   Foot Works with Resistance

a. *Flex and Point:* Sit on floor as in F-4, Foot Works, with right leg stretched straight in front, knee facing ceiling, and left leg bent comfortably in front. With friend or parent holding outstretched foot, flex foot while partner gently pulls against it to give resistance. (Partner should pull hard enough to make you work, but not so hard as to make flexing impossible.) Now point foot while partner pushes against ball of foot to give resistance. Repeat flex and point against resistance eight times. Move on to next part of exercise before changing feet.

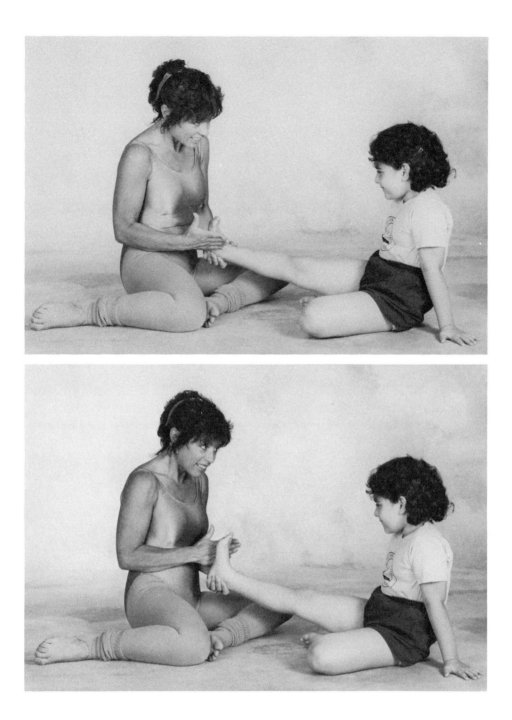

b. *In and Out:* Again as in F-4, keep right leg straight with knee facing ceiling, and left leg bent comfortably in front. This time, partner's hand is placed against inside edge of foot, close to ball. Twist foot inward against resistance. Next, partner's hand is placed on outside edge of foot, close to ball. Twist foot outward against resistance. Repeat in and out against resistance eight times. Now change feet, left leg outstretched, right bent comfortably in front, and repeat entire sequence (Flex and Point, and In and Out) with left foot.

THE LAST COOL-DOWN ROUTINE:

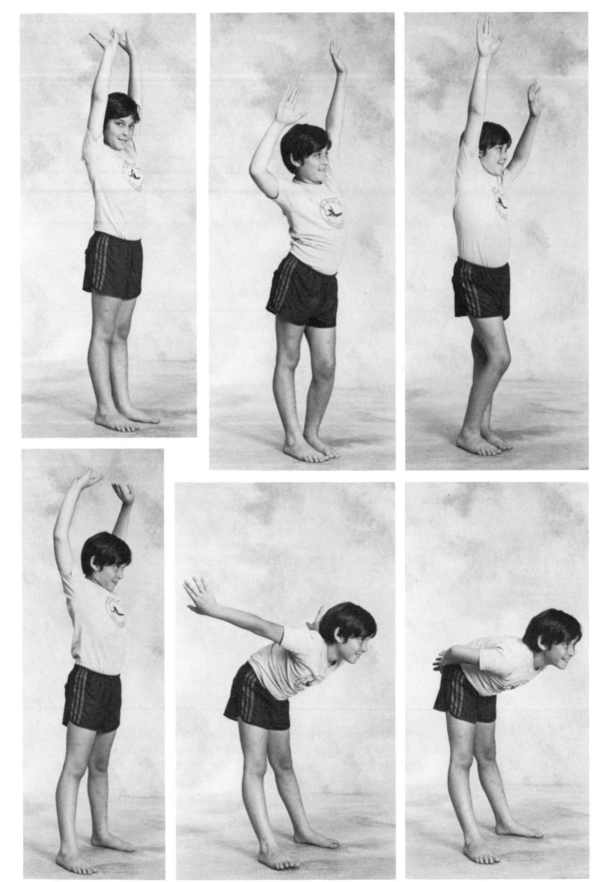

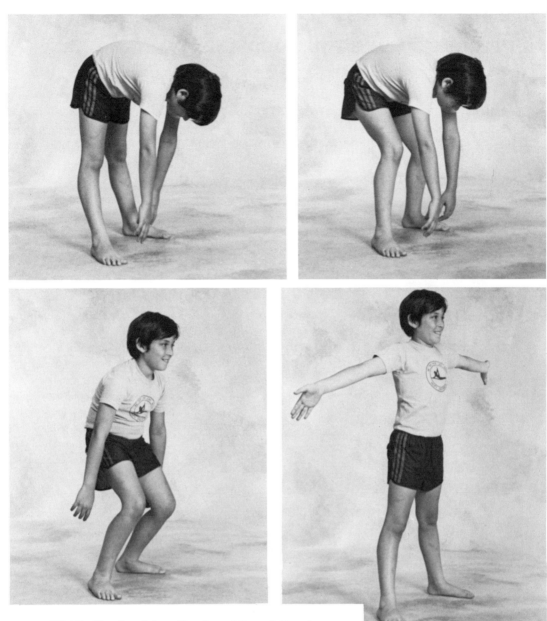

FL-20 Overhead Arm Reach and Stretch Routine

Stand with legs straight, feet together, and arms stretched straight up above head.

a. *Bend and Stretch:* Bend left knee slightly and stretch left arm high over head. Straighten left knee and release left arm, but don't lower it. Repeat with right side. Stretch each side eight times.

b. *Feet-Apart Stretch:* Spread feet apart and arch arms over head so that palms face up and fingertips point toward each other. Do not arch back. Keep hands facing up, and lower arms outward to count of four.

c. *Back Stretch:* Stretch hands behind back and bend forward from hips.

d. *Clasp:* Clasp hands behind back and, keeping legs straight, pulse torso forward four times.

e. *Forward Droop:* Unclasp hands and, letting arms droop in front of body, pulse torso forward four times. Be sure to keep legs straight.

f. *Slow Straighten:* Bend knees. Tuck backside under. Let hands fall behind body, and slowly begin to straighten torso. Keep knees bent.

g. *Back to Beginning:* Straighten legs, and continue raising arms up. Bring feet together and start entire routine over again.

Repeat Overhead Arm Reach and Stretch two to four times.

PROGRAM B: DAYS TWO, FOUR, AND SIX

REMEMBER TO BEGIN WITH BASIC WARM-UP (PAGE 26).

SHOULDERS, UPPER BACK, HIPS, AND LEGS

NOW BEGIN WITH YOUR SHOULDER EXERCISES:

SA-18 Alternating Shoulder Circle
Stand with feet slightly apart. Rest hands at sides. Circle right shoulder forward, up, back, and down. As right shoulder reaches back position, begin to circle left shoulder forward, up, back, and down. Both shoulders should be circling at same time, although they are at different positions. Repeat for two sets of eight.

 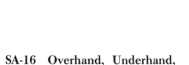

SA-16 Overhand, Underhand, Behind-Back Touch
Stand with feet slightly apart. Raise left arm up and place hand on left shoulder blade. Reach right arm behind body and place back of right hand on back. Now pull both hands toward each other as close as you can behind back. Hold two seconds and release. Change sides and repeat action. Hold two seconds. Repeat entire series two to four times. (Go slowly with this one. Do not strain.)

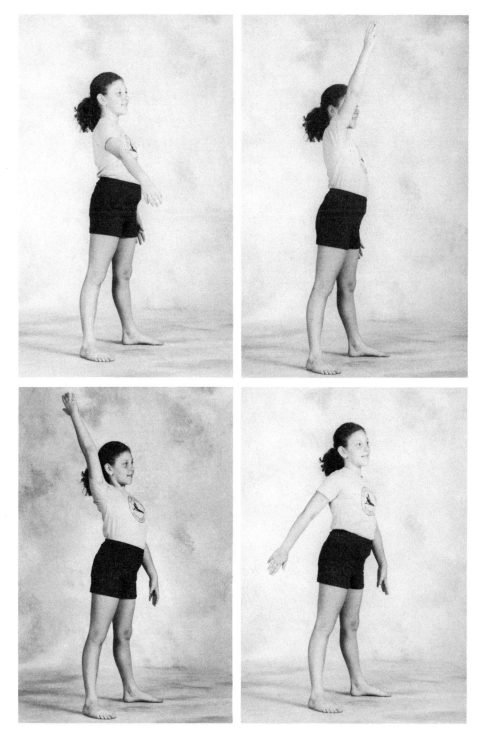

SA-6 Arm Circle

Stand with feet slightly apart, hands resting at sides. Keeping arms straight, circle right arm forward, up, back, and down eight times. Do same sequence with left arm. Now circle right arm back, up, forward, and down eight times. Repeat exercise with left arm. Perform forward circle with both arms eight times. Finally perform backward circle with both arms eight times.

SA-17 Long Island Sound Swim

Stand with feet apart. Bend forward at hips. Keeping legs straight, stretch right arm forward and out to left. Palm should face right. Now slowly move right hand to right as if pushing away something that is in water in front of you. Let body follow hand all the way to right. Stretch left arm forward and to right. Palm should face left. Slowly move left hand to left as if pushing away something that is in water in front of you. Again, let your body follow hand to left. Repeat action with alternate arms for two sets of eight.

NOW MOVE YOUR HIPS:

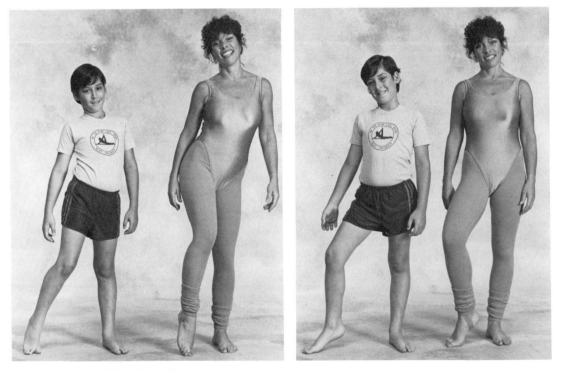

H-5 Hip Lift

Stand with feet slightly apart. Rest hands at sides. Lean weight on left leg, keeping it straight. Bend right knee and, turning right thigh slightly inward, lift hip upward. Lower hip and turn knee slightly outward. Repeat four times. Change sides and repeat exercise. Repeat entire series two to four times.

H-2   Hip Wag

Stand with feet apart. Rest hands at sides. Bend left knee, keep right leg straight, and push right hip to right. Bend right knee, straighten left leg, and push left hip to left. Get a rhythm going and wag hips from side to side. Repeat for two sets of eight.

F-8   Feet-Apart Heel Lift

Stand with feet apart. Rest hands at sides. Lean weight slightly onto left leg. Bend right knee and raise right heel off floor. Ball of right foot should be resting on floor. Hold two seconds. Straighten leg and return heel to floor. Lean weight slightly onto right leg. Bend left knee and raise left heel off floor. Hold two seconds. Stand straight again. Repeat eight times.

AND THEN ADD SOME FLEXIBILITY EXERCISES: **Standing Forward Pulse with Straight Back** (FL-1, PAGE 60) and **Standing Alternate Toe Touch** (FL-3, PAGE 52).

AND A NEW ONE:

FL-19   Alternate Elbow to Knee Touch
Stand with feet apart. Rest hands at sides. Bend right knee and twist torso down to touch left elbow to right knee. Stretch right arm outward. Straighten right knee and bend left knee while twisting body in other direction. Touch right elbow to left knee. Stretch left arm outward. Twist back and forth for two sets of eight.

GO BACK TO MORE HIP EXERCISES. THIS TIME GET DOWN ON HANDS AND KNEES.

H-4 On-Knees Straight Leg Lift (to the Side)
Get on hands and knees. Stretch right leg straight out to side with foot resting on floor. Now raise and lower straight right leg four times. Return to starting position and straighten left leg out to side. Raise and lower four times. Repeat entire series two to four times. Again avoid the burn. If this exercise becomes painful, stop and come back to it later.

H-3 On-Knees Hydrant
Get on hands and knees. Raise bent right leg out to side and hold for two seconds. Now straighten right leg out to side, keeping hip down. Hold two seconds. Return to raised bent-knee position and hold two seconds. Finally place knee back on floor again. Repeat same exercise with left leg and do entire series two more times. (If legs or backside begin to burn—hurt—during this exercise, stop and do exercise again later. This exercise, on hands and knees, is something to build up to, not to take by storm all at once. Stretching out both legs is a good way to release pain, strain, or tightness in leg muscles. To do this, place hands on floor and squat with both feet slightly wider apart than shoulder width and as far from hands as is comfortable. Now straighten legs and slowly thrust backside into air. Rock backward and forward, gently stretching backs of legs.)

WHILE STILL ON HANDS AND KNEES, MOVE ON TO UPPER BACK EXERCISES.

B-12 On-Knees Push-up

Get on hands and knees and form square with body, using floor as base. Keeping hands under shoulders, lower chest and chin to floor. Keep backside in air. Return to starting position and repeat four times.

B-13 On-Knees Alternate Arm Reach
Get on hands and knees and lower body close to knees. Reach forward as far as possible with left hand while reaching backward as far as possible with right hand. Change sides, reaching forward with right hand and backward with left. Get a rhythm going and repeat eight times.

B-10 Donkey Kick
Get on hands and knees. Keep arms straight. Lower head, and bring right knee in as close as possible toward nose. Lift head. Straighten and lift leg out behind body. Repeat four times. Change legs and repeat exercise. Perform entire sequence twice.

B-9 Paint the Wall

Get on hands and knees. Bend left arm slightly and stretch right arm straight under torso. Swing right arm out and up above back. Repeat four times, and change arms for four more repetitions.

LIE DOWN ON STOMACH FOR NEXT EXERCISES:

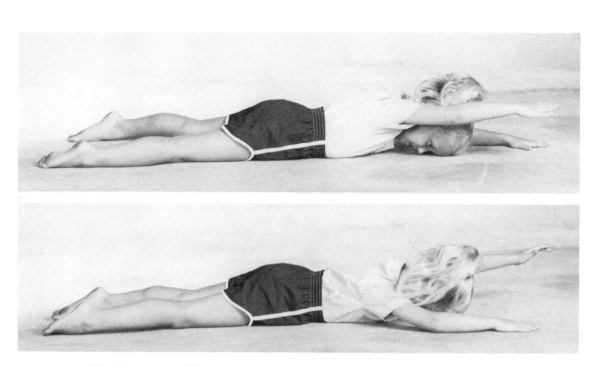

B-3 Prone Arm Lifts

Lie on stomach with legs outstretched. Stretch arms straight above head. Keep face on or near floor. Raise straight right arm up, then lower it. Be sure to keep arm close to ear. Raise straight left arm up and lower it. Keep it close to ear. Do entire sequence eight times.

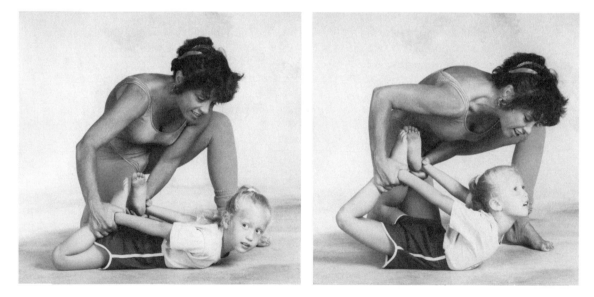

B-4 Rocking Horse

Lie on stomach. Bend knees. Clasp ankles with hands. Keep legs bent and ankles clasped, and stretch feet toward ceiling. Pull chest and thighs off floor. Hold four seconds and release. Repeat four times.

AND NOW RETURN TO HANDS AND KNEES AGAIN AND DO **Cat and Horse** (B-11, PAGE 50).

THEN SIT AND DO THE FOLLOWING FLEXIBILITY EXERCISES:

FL-16　Toes to Nose
Sit on floor with soles of feet touching. Grasp right foot with both hands and pull it up toward nose. Hold two seconds. Return foot to floor. Repeat with left foot. Perform entire series eight times.

DO SOME LEG EXERCISES BEFORE CONTINUING WITH THE UPPER BACK:

L-2　Side Leg Lifts, Big and Small
a. *Small:* Lie on right side. Rest on right elbow and forearm with legs outstretched. Keep legs straight. Point toes. Keep top of foot facing forward. Raise and lower left leg twelve inches from floor, sixteen times.
b. *Big:* Next turn top of foot out, facing ceiling. Keep toes pointed and legs straight. Raise and lower leg as high as possible. Repeat eight times.
　Then repeat entire series (small and big) lying on left side.

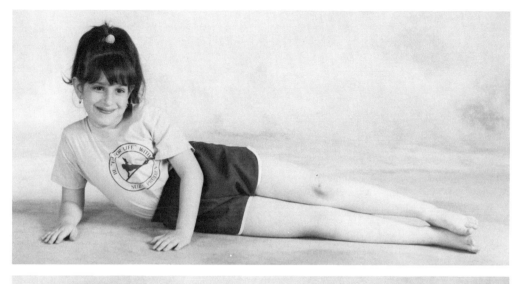

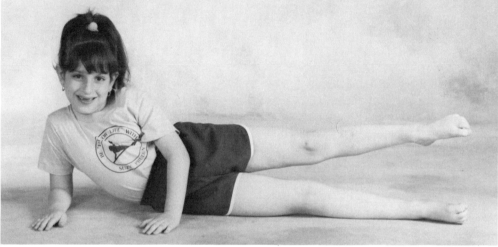

L-9 Forward Lunge
Stand with feet together. Rest hands at sides. Move right foot forward as far as comfortable. Bend right knee and lower body until you are in "lunge" position. Keep left leg straight and rest on ball of left foot. Place hands on floor in front of body. Hold position for four seconds and return to standing. Repeat, lunging left leg forward. Hold four seconds. Do entire series four times.

L-1 Lower Leg Lift
Lie on right side. Rest on right elbow and forearm with legs outstretched. Place left hand on floor in front of body. Raise left leg two feet off floor. Hold left leg in air. Raise and lower right leg to meet left leg eight to sixteen times, doing as many as you can. Turn over and repeat eight to sixteen times on left side.

TIME FOR A NEW FLEXIBILITY EXERCISE:

FL-10 L-shaped Body
Lie on right side. Lean on right elbow and forearm. Bend right leg slightly. Bend left leg, bringing knee toward shoulder. Keep left arm on inside of leg. Clasp sole of foot with left hand (thumb resting on heel). Hold on to foot. Raise leg straight into air. Hold two seconds and bend leg. Do this eight times on each side. *(Important: If it is not possible to straighten leg while holding on to foot, clasp ankle or calf.)*

NOW FOR MORE LEG EXERCISES:

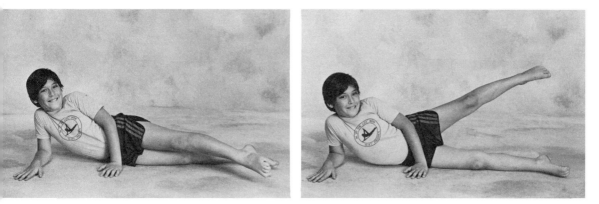

L-10 On-Side Leg Swing and Circle
a-1. *Swing:* Lie on right side with torso propped up on elbow and forearm. Rest left hand on floor in front of body. Legs should be straight and feet pointed. Raise left leg four inches off floor. Swing left leg forward, then back, keeping it straight. Repeat once more. Be sure to hold torso still.
a-2. *Forward Circle:* Without lowering leg, make two forward circles, moving leg in counterclockwise direction, forward, up, back, and down.
    Do entire series (swing and forward circle) twice and change sides. Repeat series twice lying on left side, with right leg, which will be moving in a clockwise direction to go forward, up, back, and down.
b-1. *Swing:* Return to right side. Raise left leg four inches off floor. Swing left leg backward, then forward, keeping it straight. Repeat twice. Be sure to hold torso still.
b-2. *Backward Circle:* Without lowering left leg, make two backward circles, moving leg in clockwise direction—back, up, forward, and down.
    Do entire series twice and change sides. Repeat series twice on left side with right leg, which will be moving in counterclockwise direction—back, up, forward, and down.

L-7 Pony

a. *Run:* Rest on hands and feet. Keep arms straight and buttocks in air. Run in place with feet. Do sixteen times.

b. *Hop:* Rest on hands and feet. Keep feet together, arms and legs straight, and buttocks in air. Hop in place eight times.

c. *Jump:* Rest on hands and feet. Keep buttocks in air. Bend knees and jump feet into air to touch buttocks. Repeat eight times.

STRETCH OUT AND RELEASE LEG MUSCLES WITH **Standing Forward Pulse with Round Back** (FL-2, PAGE 51).

L-8 Squat Jump

Squat down. Keep heels on floor. Rest hands on floor in front of body. Leap as high as possible. Return to squat position. Repeat four times.

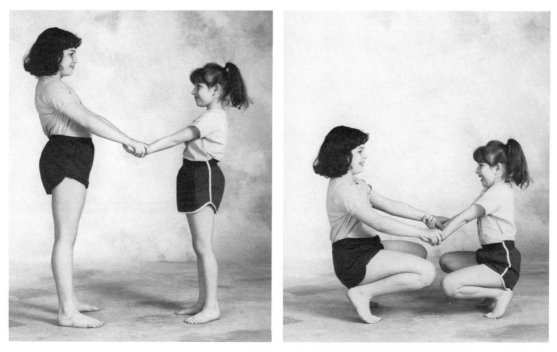

L-6 Partner Knee Bends

Face partner. Stand with feet apart. Clasp hands. Keep arms and back straight and abdominals tight. Bend knees and lower into squat position. Allow heels to come off floor. Stand straight again. Repeat eight times.

NOW RETURN TO UPPER BACK AND SHOULDERS:

L-5 Side Knee Bend and Stretch

Stand with feet apart and hands on hips, keeping abdominals tight. Bend left knee halfway down. Now bend over left leg. Grasp ankle with both hands, or dangle fingertips to touch floor by left foot. Straighten left leg and hold for four seconds. Return to starting position. Do this four times and change sides for four sequences. Again repeat entire exercise four times on each side.

B-1 Snap and Stretch

Stand with feet apart, legs straight, and abdominals tight. Raise bent elbows to shoulder height. Touch fingertips in front of chest. Keep arms bent and at shoulder height, and snap backward as far as comfortable. Bring hands forward again to meet in front of chest. Open arms outward, turning palms up and keeping arms at shoulder height. Stretch them back as far as comfortable. Repeat snap and stretch for two sets of eight.

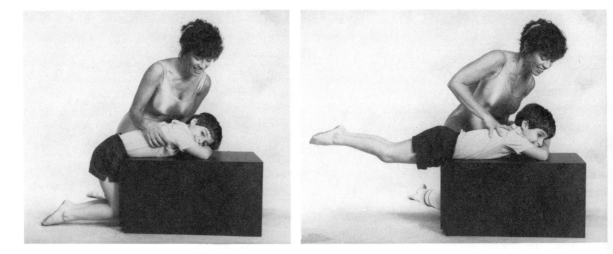

B-17 Prone Leg Lifts on Bench

Rest entire upper body, arms, and head on bench or table. Allow legs to dangle to floor. Have someone hold upper back down for support. Lift and stretch legs up and out behind body. Hold them straight out for four seconds. Lower legs and rest. Repeat four times.

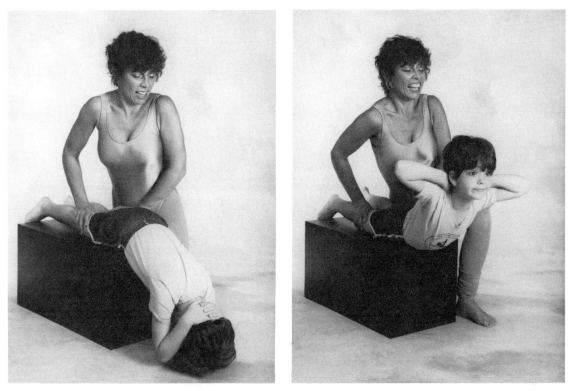

B-16 Upper Body Lifts on Bench
Rest lower body on bench. Have someone hold down thighs. Lean off bench, dangling upper body toward floor. Place hands behind neck. Lift head, chest, shoulders, and arms. Arch back like a ship's prow. Hold four seconds. Lower upper body and rest. Repeat four times.

B-15 Weightless Butterfly
Stand with feet apart. Keep back straight and raise straight arms back and above head. Swing arms down and forward to cross in front of stomach. Repeat eight times.

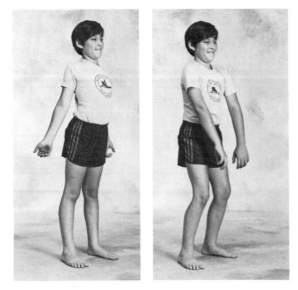

B-14 Standing, Round and Open Shoulders Using Arms

Stand with feet apart. Rest hands at sides. Do not allow back to arch. Keeping back straight, push shoulders back. Turn palms out and stretch arms slightly behind body. Hold two seconds. Twist arms under and bring them forward while rounding shoulders forward. Hold two seconds. Repeat eight times.

RETURN TO FLEXIBILITY EXERCISES:

MB-6 Dowel Overhead Arm and Chest Stretch

Stand with feet apart. Hold three-foot, three-quarter-inch dowel at each end with both hands. Keep legs straight. Do not arch back. Raise dowel above head. Slowly lower it behind body as far as comfortable. Hold for two seconds and return to front position. Repeat four times. (With practice, you will be able to lower dowel farther and farther. Do not force it; go only as far as is comfortable.)

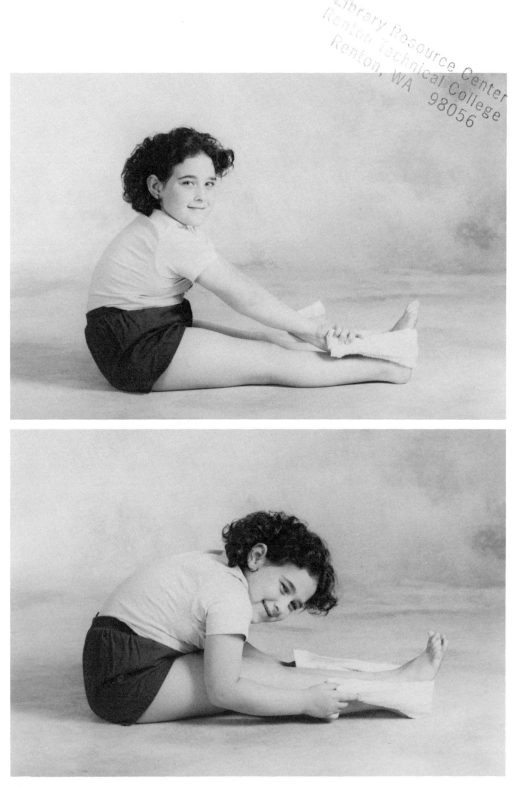

FL-12 Sitting Straight-Leg Forward Pull with Towel

Sit with feet together and legs stretched out in front of body. Clasp each end of dish towel or hand towel with both hands. Loop towel around soles of feet. Keep legs straight and pull torso forward. Release again. Do not release towel—just the tension. Repeat for two sets of eight.

HOW TO CREATE A FITNESS PROGRAM 103

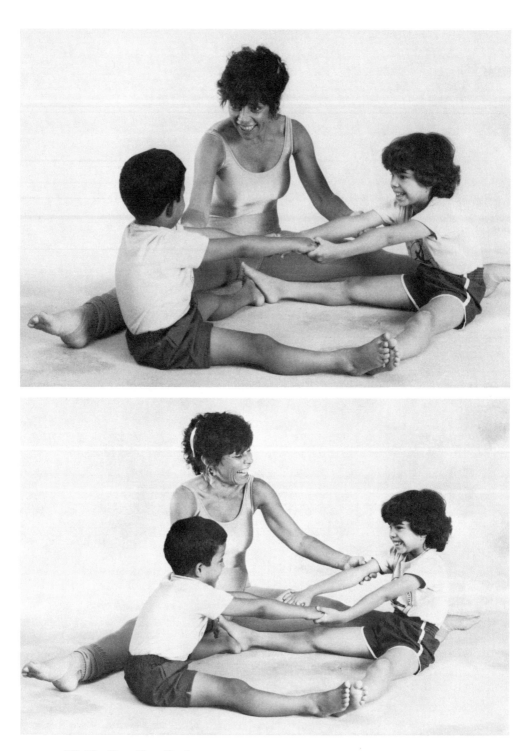

FL-13 Row Your Boat
Sit facing partner with legs straight and feet apart. Place feet against partner's. Hold hands. Keep legs straight. Partner A leans back, gently pulling Partner B forward as far as comfortable. Now reverse action, Partner B leaning back, gently pulling Partner A forward as far as comfortable. Repeat for a total of twelve times.

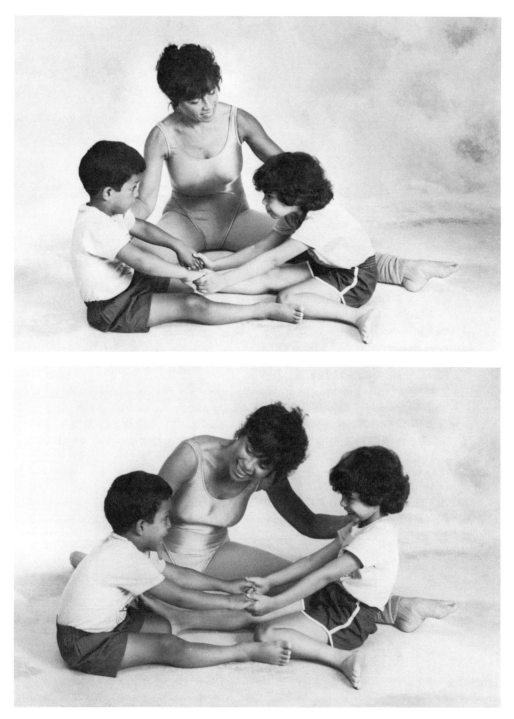

FL-14 Bent-Knee Row Your Boat

Sit facing partner with right leg straight and left leg bent. Rest left foot outside next to buttocks. Place right foot on partner's left knee and hold hands. Keep right leg straight, and as in FL-13, Row Your Boat, rock back and forth as far as comfortable, eight times. Change legs, straightening left leg and bending right. Repeat rocking eight times.

FL-11   Shoulder-Stand Leg Lower
Lie on back with arms straight at sides. Raise legs straight up, supporting lower back
with hands. Body weight will be on shoulders and upper arms. Tighten abdominal
and buttock muscles. Slowly lower legs over head toward floor. Keeping legs straight,
lower them until they are parallel to floor. Raise them again and repeat eight times.

ALTHOUGH YOU DID THE FOLLOWING EXERCISES IN PROGRAM A, FINISH
THIS PROGRAM WITH THEM. THEY ARE FOR THE LOWER BACK AND ARE
VERY IMPORTANT: **Arch and Flatten** (B-5, PAGE 47) and **Back-Flat Leg Lower** (B-7,
PAGE 48).

PROGRAM C-2: DAYS TWO, FOUR, AND SIX

MORE WEIGHTS, RESISTANCE, AND COORDINATION AND ENDURANCE

W-6   Marionette
Strap one- or two-pound weights around wrists or hold a one- or two-pound dumbbell in each hand, and stand with feet slightly apart. Bend elbows, raising upper arms to shoulder height. Dangle lower arms. Raise hands outward so arms are straight and parallel to floor. Hold three seconds and lower arms to sides. Repeat eight times.

W-7   Arm Swings
Hold one- or two-pound dumb-bells in both hands with arms at sides and hands facing inward. Stand with feet slightly apart. Keeping hips still, alternate arms, swinging them forward and back for two sets of eight.

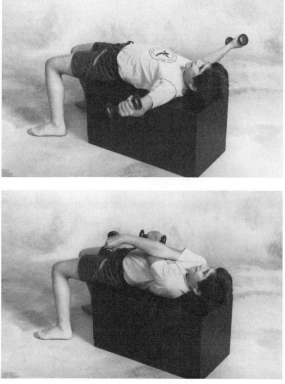

W-9 Supine Weighted Crossovers

Lie on back on bench. Hold one- or two-pound dumbbells in both hands, keeping arms at sides. Lift straight arms straight up above chest. Hold two seconds and stretch arms straight out to sides. Now swing them around to cross abdomen. Raise again. Repeat six times.

TIME FOR A NEW FLEXIBILITY EXERCISE:

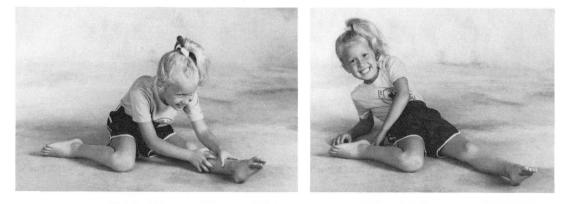

FL-9 Hamstring Psoas Stretch

Sit on floor with left leg stretched out in front. Bend right leg to side. Rest right heel close to buttocks. Keep left leg straight. Grasp ankle, pulling torso forward. Hold two seconds. Lean back to right. Rest right elbow and forearm on floor. Hold two seconds. Repeat series four times. Change sides, straightening right leg in front. Bend left leg to side. Do four. Repeat entire series twice.

NOW BACK TO WEIGHTS:

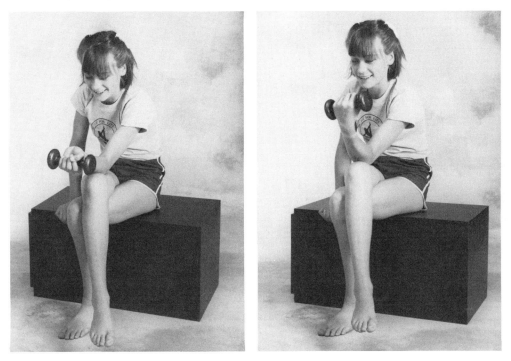

W-11   Sitting Biceps Curl

Sit on chair or bench. Hold one- or two-pound dumbbell in left hand, resting left elbow on right leg, which is crossed over left leg. With palm facing up, raise and lower left hand from leg to shoulder. Repeat eight times. Change hands. Hold dumbbell in right hand, resting right elbow on crossed left leg. With palm facing up, raise and lower right hand eight times. Repeat entire exercise twice.

W-12   Seated Straight-Arm Lifts

Hold one- or two-pound dumbbells in both hands. Sit on bench or chair. Stretch arms out to sides with palms facing up. Raise straight arms slowly above head, then lower to shoulder height. Repeat eight times.

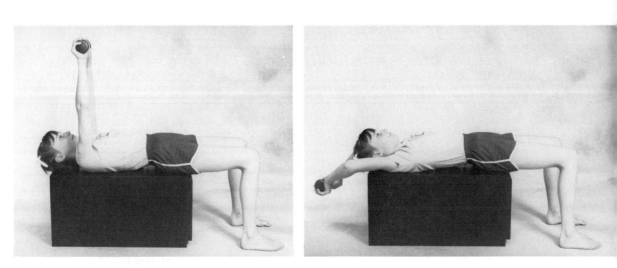

W-14 Supine Overhead Arm Swing
Lie on back on bench. Hold a one- or two-pound dumbbell with a hand at each end and raise arms straight above chest. Lower arms over head, bending elbows slightly and lowering hands toward floor. Return hands to position above chest. Repeat eight times.

W-15 Alternate Straight-Arm Lift
Stand with feet slightly apart and hold one- or two-pound dumbbells in both hands. At medium speed, raise right arm straight above head. While lowering right arm, raise left arm above head. Keep the rhythm even and at medium speed. Repeat alternate arm lifts for two sets of eight.

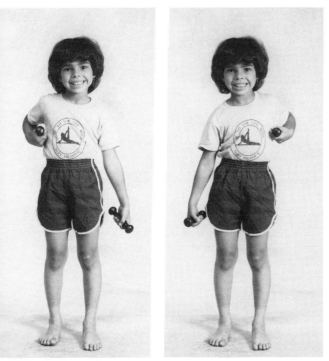

W-16   Alternate Bent-Arm Lift
Stand with feet slightly apart. Hold one- or two-pound dumbbells in both hands. Bend right elbow outward and lift right hand up to armpit. Lower right hand and lift left hand up to armpit. Work up to two sets of eight on each side.

RETURN TO A FAMILIAR FLEXIBILITY EXERCISE: **Standing Forward Pulse with Round Back** (FL-2, PAGE 51). THEN CONTINUE:

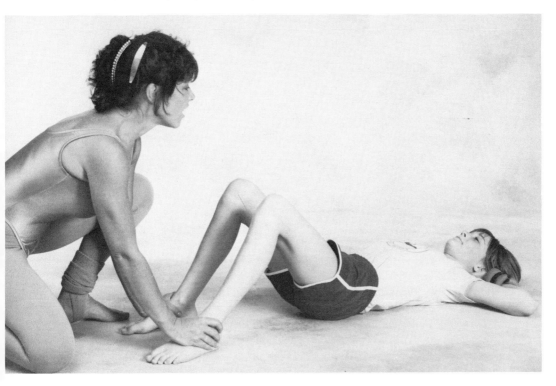

W-17 Weighted Sit-ups

(Important: If you cannot do a sit-up with your hands behind your neck, you should not attempt a weighted sit-up. See Sit-ups (A-1, page 34) for more information.)

a. *Basic:* Wrap one- or two-pound wrist weight around each wrist. Lie on back with knees bent and hands clasped behind neck. Have someone hold down feet, or place feet under couch or chair. Slowly roll up to sitting position. Slowly roll down again. Repeat for one or two sets of eight, if possible.

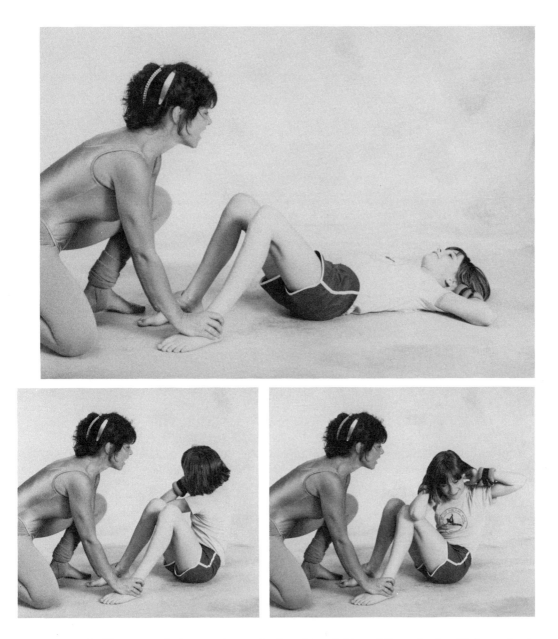

b. *Crossovers:* As in exercise *a*, attach wrist weights and lie on back with knees bent, feet resting on floor, and hands clasped behind neck. Have someone hold down feet, or place them under couch or chair. Roll into sitting position, crossing left elbow over right knee. Return to original position. Roll into sitting position, crossing right elbow over left knee. Return to original position. Repeat for one or two sets of eight on each side.

W-18 Weighted Prone Leg Lifts

Lie on stomach with legs outstretched, head resting on folded arms. With one- or two-pound weights strapped around both ankles, raise straight right leg off floor and lower it. Raise straight left leg off floor and lower it. Be sure to tighten abdominals and buttocks, and keep hips resting on floor. Do this eight times with each leg.

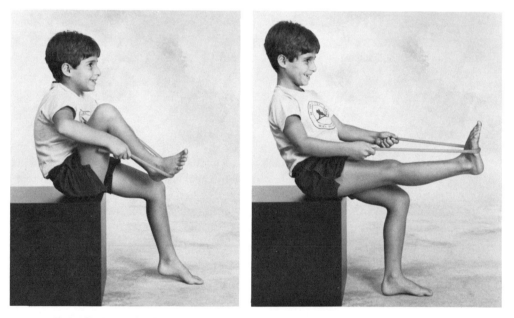

R-4 Sitting Tube Stretch with Foot

Sit on edge of chair or bench. Hold tubing at both ends or wrap it once or twice around hands to be secure. Place left foot firmly on floor while raising right foot off floor. Bring right knee up to chest. Place middle of tubing under arch of right foot. Push foot against tubing, hold hands still, and straighten leg. Hold two seconds and release. Do this eight times, change legs, and repeat eight more times.

R-5 Standing Tube Stretch with Foot

To begin this exercise, lean against wall or have parent or friend hold you for balance. Stand with feet together. Hold tubing at both ends or wrap once or twice around hands. Raise right foot and place tubing under arch. Tubing should be taut but not tight. Now straighten right leg. Hold two seconds and release. Repeat eight times. Change legs and repeat eight times.

R-6 Sitting Double Leg Tube Stretch

Do this exercise leaning against a friend or parent, or, as abdominals get stronger, just by yourself. Sit on floor. Hold tubing at both ends or wrap once or twice around hands. Tighten abdominals and raise both knees up toward chest. Place tubing under soles of feet. The tubing should be taut but not tight. Straighten legs out until tubing is tight. Hold two seconds. Release. Repeat eight times.

NOW ANOTHER FLEXIBILITY EXERCISE: **Sitting, Legs Straight, Forward Pulse** (FL-7, PAGE 41).

AND NEXT WORK ON COORDINATION AND ENDURANCE:

CE-3 Runs

a. *Regular:* Run across room or yard, forward, then backward.

b. *Legs up:* Run, kicking legs up in front of body. Lean back slightly. Be sure to tighten abdominals. Run across room or yard.

c. *Legs back:* Run, kicking legs straight out behind. Tighten abdominals, lean forward, and run across room or yard.

CE-4 Jumps

a. *Small:* Stand with feet slightly apart. Keeping jumps small, jump across room or yard.

b. *Big:* Stand with feet slightly apart. Jump as far as possible. Jump across room or yard.

CE-7 Jump-Hop

Stand with feet together. Tighten abdominals. Jump forward, landing on both feet. Jump forward, landing on left foot. Jump forward, landing on both feet again. Jump forward, landing on right foot. Continue across floor or yard.

CE-8 Jackrabbit Hop

Squat with feet apart. Jump up and out as high as possible and return to squat position. Travel across floor or yard, jumping like this.

RETURN TO **Standing Forward Pulse with Straight Back** (FL-1, PAGE 60). THEN CONTINUE WITH:

CE-9 Little-Big

This can be done with a partner or alone. Squat down with feet and knees together. Rest hands on floor or ground. Jump up, landing with feet apart and arms outstretched. Jump back into squat position. Repeat eight times.

CE-10 Little-Big Turn

Squat down with feet and knees together. Rest hands on floor or ground. Jump up and turn to right. Land with feet apart and arms outstretched. Jump back to squat position, turning to face forward again. Jump and turn to left. Land with feet apart and arms outstretched. Jump and return to forward squat position. Repeat sequence for a total of eight times.

CE-13 Twist Jump
Stand with feet together, arms outstretched at shoulder height. Hold torso still and face forward. Jump in place, turning knees and feet to left and bending left arm. Jump in place, turning knees and feet to right and bending right arm. Jump first left, then right, sixteen times.

HERE'S A NEW FLEXIBILITY EXERCISE:

FL-4 Bottoms Up
Stand with feet together and hands at sides. Squat down and put hands on floor in front of body. Allow heels to come up off floor. Keeping fingertips on floor, slowly straighten legs. Place heels on floor and lift buttocks into air. Hold four seconds and return to squat position. Repeat sequence eight times.

NOW ADD THESE EXERCISES FROM PROGRAM C-1: **Monkey Walk** (CE-14, PAGE 75) AND **Wheelbarrow** (CE-15, PAGE 75). MOVE ON AND USE SOME NEW EQUIPMENT:

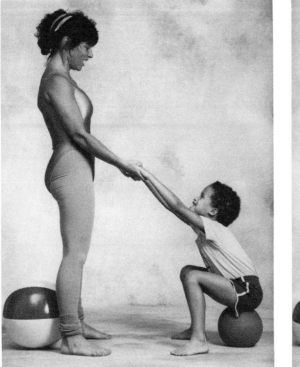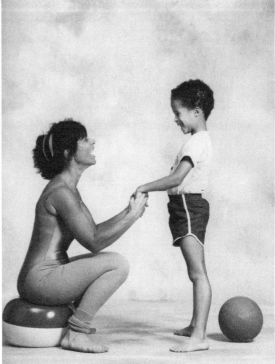

E-2 Ball Squat
Stand facing partner, holding hands. Place beach ball or basketball directly behind each partner. Partner A squats down to sit lightly on his ball. As partner A stands up again, Partner B sits lightly on his ball. Get a rhythm going and alternate sitting and standing sixteen times.

E-4 Through the Hoop
(This exercise uses a Hula-Hoop as a jump rope. It may be easier for smaller children than using a jump rope because the rope can collapse and the hoop can't.)

Stand straight in center of hoop, holding one side up with both hands. Using hands and wrists to turn hoop, swing it up over head and down in front. Allow hoop to shift through your hands as you turn it. As hoop reaches foot level, jump over it. Get a rhythm going and work up to 24 jumps.

120

E-5 Hoop Hopscotch

Place a series of three to twelve hoops on floor. Alternate pattern so that it looks like a hopscotch board. Start at one end and jump into single hoop with both feet, feet together. Jump into double hoops, landing on both feet with one foot in each hoop. Jump into next single hoop with feet together, landing on both feet.

Variation 1: Using three hoops, jump into first hoop with feet together. Jump into double hoops with feet apart, one foot in each hoop. Perform turning jump in midair to face opposite direction and land with right foot in hoop that left foot had been in, left foot in hoop that right foot had been in. Jump to hoop one, landing on both feet. Repeat three times.

Variation 2: Using three hoops, hop into first hoop with right foot. Jump with both feet into double hoops. Perform turning jump in midair so that each foot lands in hoop other foot had been in. Hop back into single hoop on left foot and hop out. Repeat three times.

Variation 3: Using more than three hoops, hop on right foot in first single hoop. Jump with both feet into double hoops. Hop onto left foot in next single hoop and continue. Hop out and repeat three times.

AND FINISH WITH A GOOD FLEXIBILITY STRETCH: **Feet Apart, Bottoms Up, and Chest Stretch** (FL-18, PAGE 77). MOVE ON TO PROGRAM D NOW, BEFORE YOU COOL DOWN (SEE THE FOLLOWING TARGETED EXERCISES).

PROGRAM D: TARGETED EXERCISES

GYMNASTICS EQUIPMENT, EYE-HAND COORDINATION, AEROBICS, SPORTS-SPECIFIC EXERCISES

GYMNASTICS EQUIPMENT

(Note to parents: Before ending the exercise program daily, be sure to include some exercises using gymnastics equipment. Add these to the program as you get equipment. A balance beam may be the only thing you have difficulty making. It is not important to have a regulation beam; a two-by-four raised a few inches off the floor will do adequately. Be sure that the wide side of the board is facing the ceiling. Also be sure to brace the two-by-fours so that they're sturdy. Any two- or three-inch-wide, foot-long pieces of wood nailed crossways to the underside of the beam will stabilize it. Use nails long enough to hold the braces and short enough not to come through the top of the piece of wood. Sand and paint wood so surface is smooth and splinter-free.

(When you are working with equipment, it is important to remember to "spot" your child. This means standing in a manner that allows you to catch him if he begins to lose his balance and fall. Spotting does not mean hovering over him as if he's going to fall any minute. It is very important that you are there for his safety and that he knows he is protected. It is also very important that he does not feel stifled and overprotected. Remember that children can sense your fear, so if you have any apprehensions while your child is on the equipment, let someone else spot him.)

GE-1 Balance Beam Walk

Stand at one end of balance beam. Raise arms out to sides and tighten buttocks and abdominals. Walk across beam. *(Note:* The abdominals and buttocks are important in maintaining balance. This will become particularly evident on a beam.)

GE-2 Backward Balance Beam Walk

Stand at one end of balance beam with arms stretched comfortably out to sides at shoulder height. Tighten buttocks and abdominals. Slowly walk backward.

GE-3 Step Kick

Stand at one end of balance beam. Tighten buttocks and abdominals. Extend arms out to sides at shoulder height. Step forward on left foot. Keeping right leg straight, kick it forward into air as high as comfortably possible. Step down onto beam with right foot. Kick left foot into air. Go across beam in this manner. (*Note:* Initially kicks may be low. That's fine. Work up to higher kicks as they become possible.)

GE-4 Balance Beam Squat Walk

Squat down at one end of balance beam. Raise hands out to sides and tighten buttocks and abdominals. Stay in squat position and walk across beam.

GE-5 Wheelbarrow
Place both hands on one end of balance beam. With someone holding up legs parallel with beam, walk across beam on hands. Do not allow back to sag.

GE-6 Monkey Walk
Stand on hands and feet at one end of balance beam. Keeping buttocks up, walk across beam.

MOVE ON TO EYE-HAND COORDINATION:

EYE-HAND COORDINATION

(Note to parents: Eye-hand coordination exercises are the answer to a young child's statement "I'm bored" or "I don't have anything to do." There are many old-fashioned children's games that one might not think of as exercise, or even as valuable. Children love them, and they have benefits far beyond what we imagined. Games such as jacks and the old pat-a-cake hand patterns are examples of these. They are particularly good for eye-hand coordination, and they enhance self-motivation and self-discipline.)

EH-1 Jacks
Sit comfortably on floor and try these variations.
a. *The Flip:* Take the jacks in your most coordinated hand. Bunch them close together and practice tossing them up, just a little bit. Catch as many as you can on the back of your hand. Toss them up again and catch them in the palm of your hand. This strategy is designed to limit the number of single jacks you need to pick up. It's possible to play a whole game simply by flipping. This is such a valuable coordination exercise it's a good idea to practice with each hand.
b. *Plain and Simple:* Take the jacks in your most coordinated hand and flip them. Reserve the jacks you caught in a pile outside the playing area so you can concentrate on the rest. Throw the ball in the air, allowing it to bounce once before catching it while picking up one jack, and then repeat to pick up the remaining jacks. Don't touch any of the other jacks while picking up the one you intended to pick up, and don't let the ball bounce a second time, or you'll have to start over! When you've picked up all the jacks, toss them out again, and this time pick up two at a time without moving any other jacks. Then it's three, four, and so on, until you've picked up all the jacks at once.

All jacks games involve picking up the jacks in progressive numerical sequences: ones, twos, threes, and so on. Here are some other variations you can try.
c. *Around the World:* Toss the ball up, pick up the jacks, and make a large circle around the ball with your hand before you catch it.
d. *No-Bounce Ball:* Toss the ball, pick up the jacks, and catch the ball before it bounces.
e. *Uncoordinated Hand:* Play jacks with the hand you usually don't use.
f. *Clap One:* Toss the ball in the air, clap once, pick up the jacks, and catch the ball.
g. *Clap Two:* Toss the ball in the air, clap twice, pick up the jacks, and catch the ball. You can add as many claps as you can possibly do as you get better.
h. *Pigs in a Blanket:* Throw the ball in the air, pick up the jacks, transfer the jacks to your other hand, and then catch the ball.
i. *Combination:* Try combining Around the World and Pigs in a Blanket, making a big circle around the ball with your hand, then transferring the jacks to your other hand before catching the ball.

You can make up any variety of games with jacks: pat the top of your head, rub your stomach, change position on the floor—anything you want to do.

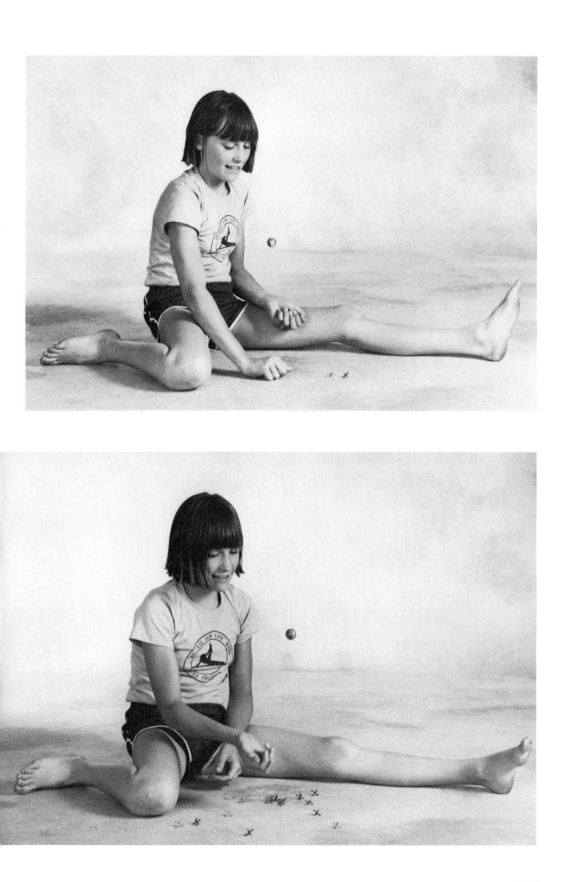

EH-2 Pat-a-Cake
Here are two relatively simple rhythms and hand motions. There are many more. Sit or kneel opposite a partner and try them.

Pat-a-	Slap both thighs with palms, right to right, left to left.
cake,	Clap hands together.
Pat-a-	Clap each other's right hand (cross).
cake,	Clap hands together.
bak-	Clap each other's left hand (cross).
er's	Clap hands together.
man,	Clap each other's hands, right to left, left to right (no cross).
(pause)	Clap hands together.
Bake	Slap thighs with palms, right to right, left to left.
me a	Clap hands together.
cake	Clap each other's right hand (cross).
as	Clap hands together.
fast	Clap each other's left hand (cross).
as you	Clap hands together.
can,	Clap each other's hands, right to left, left to right (no cross).
(pause)	Clap hands together.

Roll it	Place right hand opposite stomach, palm facing stomach, place left hand directly behind it. Make rolling motion.
and pat it,	Turn left palm up. Pat left palm with palm of right hand.
and mark it with D,	Describe large *D* in air in front of you.
And put it in the oven for Daddy and me.	With both palms facing up, make a motion as if putting bread into a large oven.

OH, COME OUT, PLAYMATE

Oh, *come* out, *play-* (pause) *mate* (pause, *pause*),	Slap thighs with both hands (clap hands together on
Come *out* and *play* with *me* (pause, *pause*),	each underlined beat), cross clap right to right,
And *bring* your *dol-* lies *three* (pause, *pause*),	(clap together), then left to left (clap together),
Climb *up* my *ap-*ple *tree* (pause, *pause*).	then clap straight across (clap together). Keep the
Slide *down* my *rain-* (pause) *bow* (pause, *pause*)	rhythm steady.
In*to* my *cel-*lar *door* (pause, *pause*),	
And *we'll* be *play-* (pause) *mates*	
For-*ev*-er *more!* For!*ev!er!more!*	Clap across left to right, right to left, on each syllable.

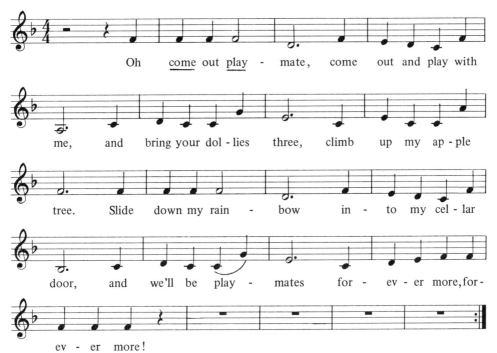

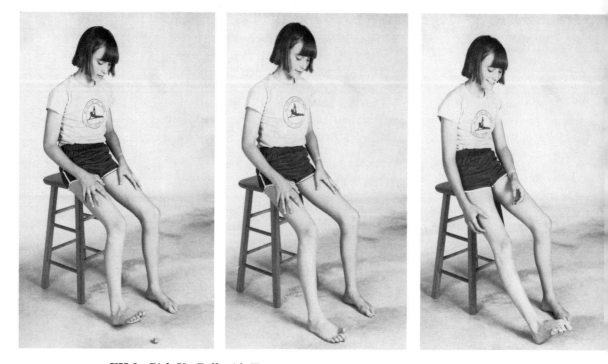

EH-3 Pick Up Ball with Toes

In bare feet, sit on stool or chair and place small ball on floor in front of feet. Pick ball up between first and second toes of right foot. Do this four times, then do four more with left foot.

EH-4 Bat the Ball

Stand with feet slightly apart and hold a lightweight plastic bat up in right hand. Have someone throw ball, and hit it with the bat. Then change hands and hit with bat in left hand. Repeat four times with each arm.

(Note to Parents: Beach balls are wonderful! Whenever a child is having difficulty with almost any ball game, use a beach ball to develop his skills and self-esteem. This is particularly good for younger children, as well as older children who are having difficulty with batting. Don't be disappointed if your child can't play regular baseball at the age of five or six. It is difficult for him at his age to coordinate gross motor movement and eye-hand coordination to the side. Once the beach ball is mastered, work up to a Nerf ball, and then on to the regulation softball.)

EH-5 Two-handed Ball Smack
Stand with feet apart and hold a bat at each end. Have someone throw a Nerf ball, and hit it with center of bat. Repeat eight times.

EH-6 Paddleball
(Use the paddleball with ball attached to paddle with rubber band.)
a. *Upright:* Stand with feet slightly apart. Hold paddle upright in right hand and hit ball as many times as possible. Build up to 100. Change hands and repeat.
b. *Horizontal:* Hold paddle with its face facing the opposite wall. Hit ball outward as many times as possible, building up to 100. Change hands and repeat.

Don't get discouraged if it takes a while even to get to two!

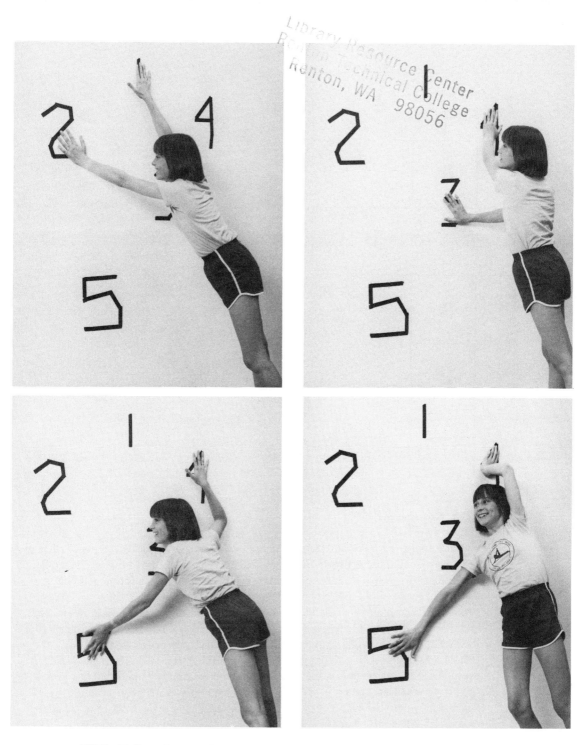

EH-7 Follow the Numbers

Place cut-out numbers randomly on a blank wall, or draw on a large sheet of paper. Stand facing numbers, and with a slow beat, steady drum or metronome keeping time, touch each number with alternating hands. When you can do this comfortably without missing a number, pick up speed.

Variation: Have someone call out numbers slowly. Touch each number called with alternating hands, no matter how far away that number may be.

HOW TO CREATE A FITNESS PROGRAM   133

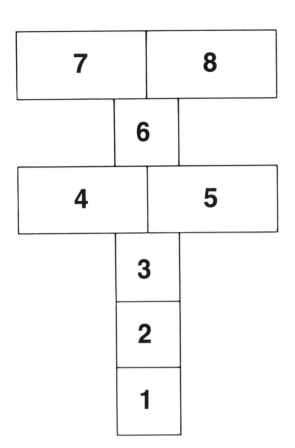

EH-8   Hopscotch

Draw a hopscotch (see diagram) with chalk on a cement sidewalk, or create it with masking tape on a basement or playroom floor. Number the boxes. In every single box, hop on one foot. In the double boxes, land on two feet, one foot in each box. Do not land on any lines. Once a player can do this back and forth, it is time to begin the game. Throw a pebble into box one. Hop over box one, landing in box two. Hop in two, hop in three, double-hop in four and five, hop in six, double-hop in seven and eight. Turn with a double hop again in seven and eight and hop back to number two. Pick up the pebble while standing on one foot. Hop out of the board. Throw the pebble into box two. Hop in one and hop over number two to three. When a player completes a round, he gets to claim a box. No one can step or hop in that box except the player who has claimed it. The rules of the game are that a player cannot hop in any box in which there is a pebble, his or any other player's, he cannot put his other foot down when he's hopping, and he cannot touch any of the lines when he's hopping. If a player does any of the above, he has to keep trying with the same box until he successfully completes the turn. The player whose pebble travels with each turn through each of the eight boxes wins.

Circle Hopscotch: Prepare the board as shown in the diagram. The principle of the game is to hop, on only one foot, all the way around the circle, from the starting box to the inside box. Every time a player completes a turn he gets to choose a box that is totally his; his name goes in it. No one can step in his box, but he can rest in it. The one who has the most boxes wins.

135

AEROBICS:

(Note to parents: Warming up and aerobic games can make up much of formal exercise. The following games are excellent for conditioning both the body and entire cardiovascular system. They enhance coordination skills, which will be increasingly important to your child as he gets along in school.)

A. *Freeze Tag*

This is a tag game in which a player unfreezes ten seconds after he is tagged. (Count slowly—one one hundred, two one hundred, etc.) He can therefore get right back into the game. Choose someone to be "it" for a specific period of time, say, three minutes, so that there is a continuous change.

B. *Garbage Ball*

Two teams, of any size more than three, play on either side of a net. Each team gets five Nerf balls to be batted (volleyball style) over the net. The side that winds up with the fewest balls at the end of a specified time period wins!

C. *Freeze Dodge Ball*

Two teams line up on either side of a line, each with five Nerf balls. Each team throws at the other simultaneously. If a player is hit, he freezes for ten seconds and then gets right back in the game. The object: not to get hit!

In addition, jumping rope, swimming, and biking are ideal aerobic activities. Encourage your kids to cycle, roller-skate, work on a pogo stick or unicycle. Let them do the programs in this book to fast music. Encourage them to work on a wooden floor, and look into getting them sneakers that protect both the metatarsals and the heels.

A word about jogging:

If you are setting up an aerobics program for children that includes jogging or running, teach them to run on the ground, not on the pavement, if possible. We ran around our backyard for years playing horse with a piece of clothesline, with no ill effects. Jogging on asphalt and cement with sneakers that are inadequate to the task of protecting metatarsal and heel bones can cause trouble. You wouldn't run a horse on asphalt without rubber shoes if you valued the horse, but people jog on cement all the time, and the result can be stress fractures, shin splints, and knee and hip damage.

Aerobic Exercise Clubs:

In Rye, New York, the teachers developed clubs to encourage the children to perform aerobic exercises (see Appendix C). They created charts on which the kids recorded each quarter mile they ran on a measured area near the school or in the playground. After each quarter-mile run, the adult supervisor signed off on the card, and when the child reached the equivalent of five miles, he became a member of the "Five-Mile Club." He could then work toward a "Ten-Mile Club" membership. (We've included some club forms below.)

The American Heart Association has developed a program for schools to access if they want to hold jump-a-thons for building cardiac strength through jumping rope. These jumping-rope marathons are great activities to include in school programs. Within your child's program you can have daily timed jumping workouts aimed toward the "Hour Club." Set it up so that your child and his friends get together to jump rope in your presence, and sign them off on a long roll sheet. As each of them reaches his goals, you can create a certificate for him and cut a small piece of ribbon for him to safety-pin to his shirt. These wonderful programs don't have to be expensive. They don't have to be limited to use by schools to be effective.

By all means encourage kids to do aerobic exercise. Aerobics are wonderful. They're beneficial, they're fun, they're what kids ought to be doing.

FIVE-MILE CLUB

Date:_____

Quarter Miles Run	Date	Adult Signature
1		
2		
3		
Mile One		
5		
6		
7		
Mile Two		
9		
10		
11		
Mile Three		
13		
14		
15		
Mile Four		

17		
18		
19		
Mile Five!		

CONGRATULATIONS ON BECOMING A MEMBER OF THE FIVE MILE CLUB! ! ! ! ! ! ! ! ! ! ! ! !

TEN-MILE CLUB

Date:_____

Quarter Miles Run	Date	Adult Signature
1		
2		
3		
Mile One		
5		
6		
7		
Mile Two		
9		
10		
11		
Mile Three		
13		
14		
15		
Mile Four		
17		
18		
19		
Mile Five		
21		
22		
23		
Mile Six		
25		
26		
27		
Mile Seven		
29		
30		

31	

Mile Eight

33	
34	
35	

Mile Nine

37	
38	
39	

Mile Ten!

CONGRATULATIONS ON BECOMING
A MEMBER OF THE TEN-MILE
CLUB!!!!!!!!!!!!!!!

SPORT-SPECIFIC EXERCISES

As we have stated before, games and sports in and of themselves do not guarantee physical fitness. Unfortunately, common belief has it that if you play games, that's enough. The child who has not had the benefits of conditioning exercises has two problems. First, he probably isn't going to play as well as he might. Second, he's a target for injury. Each sport uses different sets of muscles, which must be prepared and conditioned.

Major league baseball players begin their season long before it actually begins. They spend six to eight weeks in training camps, preparing their bodies with conditioning exercises. When their season begins, their bodies are in top physical shape. Only in this way can they remain protected and play well.

Good skiers also begin preparing their bodies long before they actually hit the slopes. In the 1950s Bonnie created the Adelpate Ski Club. During the ten-year period in which she taught a program of pre-ski exercises, not one child was seriously injured. In our experience on several ski patrols, it was the occasional skier who sat behind a desk year-round and *came to the mountain to get his exercise* who was a prime target for injury.

Sports generally break down into several general categories: spike, endurance, and a combination of both. Spike sports are those sports which predominantly call upon the body to move from the resting point to fast action without any buildup; baseball, golf, and volleyball are predominantly spike sports. Endurance sports are those which call upon the body to move continuously; aerobics, jogging, swimming, and cycling are examples of endurance sports. Skiing, basketball, football, soccer, and tennis are mixtures. Spike sports do not get you in great shape, and if you're not in great shape already, you could pull a muscle while playing them.

We've provided a sports evaluation chart with a child's progress in baseball recorded as an example. Use the chart as a guide to break down your child's sport into components. Then, with your child, go over how you both feel about how he does in each component. Write in your evaluation. Use the programs outlined earlier in this book and add those on the following pages both to remedy any specific problems and to promote general conditioning. Every month, look back at the chart to see how both of you feel he's doing now, and note the dates of improvement in the appropriate column.

SPORTS EVALUATION CHART

SPORT	EXCELLENT	GOOD	OKAY	POOR	REALLY POOR	*IMPROVED
Baseball (sample)			4/3			
Batting				4/3		5/6
Running		4/3				5/6
Catching					4/3	5/6
SPORT						

Here are some recommended programs for both categories of sports. These programs should be included in regular conditioning programs at least six weeks before taking part in a given sport.

SPIKE SPORTS

SA-1	The Swim	page 27
SA-5	The Backstroke	page 58
SA-10	Hand Walk-Forward Droop	page 61
L-3	Side-to-Side Knee Bends	page 29
L-4	Knee Bends	page 30
L-5	Side Knee Bend and Stretch	page 99

Now choose ten of your favorite flexibility exercises (see Appendix B).

B-1	Snap and Stretch	page 100
B-7	Back-Flat Leg Lower	page 48
A-1	Sit-ups	page 34
A-2	Crossover Sit-ups	page 44
A-8	Ankle Catch	page 46

And don't forget to cool down (page 78).

ENDURANCE EXERCISES

A-7	Sitting Foot Bounce	page 55
A-6	Up, Up, and Around	page 38
A-10	Lower Abdominal Lift	page 40
SA-11	Push-ups	page 60
SA-12	Chin-ups	page 62
L-7	Pony	page 98
L-8	Squat Jump	page 98

Now, choose any ten of your favorite flexibility exercises (see Appendix B).

E-1	Jump Rope	page 76
SA-14	Push a Pebble with Your Nose	page 56
W-18	Weighted Prone Leg Lifts	page 114
W-2	Shoulder Shrug	page 66
W-9	Supine Weighted Crossovers	page 108
W-15	Alternate Straight-Arm Lift	page 110

And don't forget to cool down (page 78).

5

Special Cases

There are three groups of children we are going to talk about that are outside of what is generally considered "the norm." They are the skilled child, the obese child, and the slow child. Each of these groups of children can benefit from this program in the way every other child can. This is important to know, because often we feel that skilled children don't need a program, slow children are hopeless cases, and obese children—well, obese children wouldn't like exercise anyway. That is untrue.

Some of the exercises may have to be modified slightly, but that does not mean that the child cannot do them. The skilled child will become more skilled, the obese child will be made more fit and given more self-esteem, and the slow child will gain in brain function, strength, and coordination.

THE SKILLED CHILD

If your child has star potential, it's a heady experience. You can hear the roll of the drums. You can hear the national anthem. You can see the trophies and gold medals. But ultimately, what is important is whether the push comes from you or from your child. Are you a driving parent who may drive your star into a lifetime of neurosis, or is this your child's ambition and are you supporting his efforts toward success? It's an almost invisible line. Crossing it can be catastrophic.

The star athlete is a combination of natural talent, personal drive, discipline, good training, and parental support. Without these components, the possibility of making it to the top is slender. Of the five components, the least important is parental support. That's not to say it isn't vitally important, but it's the least important. Parents don't have to be involved in supporting their child's ambition for the child to become successful. Children have been known to get to the top without any support from their parents at all. If your child doesn't have the discipline and drive to go along with his natural ability and you're pushing, all that gets created is neurosis.

The best approach to developing an athlete is to keep his participation in the sport fun and rewarding. It's important to make it possible for the child to participate as often as possible. It's important to make demands and build a discipline structure, but not to push and drive. The prayer for the parent with the talented child is:

> **Lord, give me the courage, devotion, and willingness to make the sacrifices that will support my child to the success that can be his, and give me the wisdom to know when I am supporting my own ambitions rather than his.**

There is one important thing for parents to remember: if you find you have pushed too hard, you can stop pushing. It's as simple as that. And if you have the courage, you can say to the child, "Sorry, I was pushing." You never lose face when you tell the truth to your child. It may be uncomfortable, but like everything else, it gets easier with practice. The interesting thing about this is that very soon you are no longer pushing, and even sooner, your child is attaining greater success.

Supporting a talented child takes devotion and sacrifice. It means early morning chauffeuring to ski slopes or equestrian events. It means fence judging in support of local pony clubs, or gatekeeping on frigid mountains. It means being terrified as your child begins to pit himself against personal and dangerous experiences, and not letting on. It may even mean giving up the raising of your child so that he can get the best training at a gymnastic facility far from home, or moving near a good skating rink with a first-class coach. It's joy and fear and work. And it begins when the child is very young. Most athletes on the Olympic level were introduced to their sport of choice by the time they were four or five. There are exceptions, of course, but these are few and far between.

Look at quality athletes: gymnasts are often burned out by eighteen, having reached their peak at thirteen or fourteen. Skaters mature a little later, but they often peak in their late teens or early twenties. Some track and field athletes are older. Skiers are generally older, but show their competitive promise early: skiers usually start looking good at six or seven and are racing by the fifth grade. Baseball and football players seldom last beyond their mid-thirties.

You can recognize natural athletes when they walk in the room. Athletes make every team they want to make. Give them a sport, and they can master it. They have a communication between mind and body that simply exists. Natural athletes are identifiable as infants. They have a different approach to figuring out how the body works, which you can observe as early as six or eight months. Often they are more fearless than other children. And it's a parent's job to keep them safe without killing that fearlessness.

THE OVERWEIGHT CHILD

If your child is overweight, you are already aware that overweight children get a lot of negative feedback in this country. They are often ridiculed, verbally abused, and taunted. It's hard to know who does the most damage, well-meaning adults or nasty peers. The pain and abuse suffered by the overweight child seem to be mirrored in the life of the overweight adult. Since fully a quarter of the population is now overweight, and that number seems to be growing, it's important that we address the issue.

In America today, obesity is regarded as something terrible. Children and adults alike are quick to tell the obese person that all there is to dieting is eating less (editorial comments like "you pig" may be left out, but they're there, unspoken). If dieting were as easy as simply cutting down on food, there would not be one overweight person in America. If inspirational judgments such as "You're so smart, if only you weren't so fat," were helpful, there would not be one overweight person in America. If diets actually worked, there would not be one overweight person in America. Clearly, the problem has to be looked at differently.

Overweight generally shows itself early. By the early teens a person who is going to have lifetime weight difficulty will show that tendency. There is no guarantee that a fat child is going to be a fat adult, but a fat teenager often will become one. It is now known that out of every 200 people who start a diet every year, only one successfully manages to lose and keep weight off over time. It is known that many thirteen- and fourteen-year-old girls diet regularly, and that this can adversely affect their health.

In a recent study of adipose tissue (fat cells) at Rockefeller University, it was found that brain cells and adipose cells are the two types of cells that are not cannibalized by the body in times of starvation. Once adipose cells have been developed for fat storage, they may get empty, but they do not disappear. It was further found that because of an evolutionary factor, bodies that are subjected to periodic starvation (i.e., dieting) tend to use food more efficiently so that weight loss becomes increasingly difficult. As soon as the starvation period is over, the body immediately begins storing up fat again, and dieters usually gain back twelve pounds for every ten pounds they lose.

Because it is so difficult to lose weight, it is vitally important that you teach your overweight child that he need not be limited by overweight as far as physical activity is concerned.

It is important to approach your child's teachers and make sure that the traditional American prejudice against the overweight doesn't spill over into his physical education classes. *If your child is going to be fat, let him be fit and strong, well coordinated, and flexible.*

In dealing with overweight, you must be a kind of warrior where your child is concerned. It's inexcusable that a fat or an uncoordinated child should be chosen last for a team, knocked off a team, or in any way be humiliated because of his body, but it happens all the time. It is up to the child's teachers and parents to make certain that doesn't happen. In our testing, we found that the successful school physical education programs had dropped intramural sports because they limit the number of children that can play in after-school programs. Unless he is "Refrigerator" Perry (and who knows how much *he* struggled to be allowed on the team), the fat child is usually one of the first to be cut, and he's the one who needs after-school fitness programs most. Make sure he's included. It's really up to you. If your school has a policy of exclusion, make sure you start exercising your child early so he can make the team because he's fitter than the other children. Start telling him that the exercises will help him make the team (see Affirmations, page 151). Considering the way most programs are run, and considering the general condition of most other children, it isn't difficult to give your child an edge.

It's bad enough to be handicapped by weight without being crippled by it. And there's no reason for it. Simply work with your child in the area of eye-hand coordination, spend extra time conditioning his body, and encourage him to participate in sports. It is particularly helpful to start by giving him the muscles to do well in sports.

We can tell you what doesn't work in dealing with obesity. Focusing on it and harping about it don't work. Your child knows he's overweight. Chances are he qualifies every nice thing anyone says to him with "Yeah, but I'm fat." He doesn't have to hear about his attractive face and how much better it would look if only he could lose a few pounds. If your child could lose a few pounds that easily, he would probably lose them.

Developing self-esteem in the face of being overweight does work. Finding things to like about himself despite the fact that he's overweight does work. And a plan to be fit and participate in sports is part of the self-esteem development strategy.

Some of the strategies for establishing overweight patterns start much earlier than age five. Food is so central to our culture that it's very easy to program young children toward obesity:

- Feeding an infant every time it cries teaches the child that if he wants to be cuddled or held, he has to eat.
- Rewarding children with food when they are very little creates the risk of having them associate pleasure with food.
- Force-feeding children (the old "finish everything on your plate" routine) teaches the child to override what his body is telling him about hunger and satisfaction. The overweight person usually does not experience hunger as a trigger to eating and doesn't recognize the body's normal signals for satisfaction because he's never been trained to recognize them.
- Giving a child food to "make him feel better" teaches the child to associate comfort with food.
- Praising the child when he eats, or linking food with statements such as "Eat this if you love me," also teaches the child to ignore what his body tells him.

If you have just read these statements and decided *you* did everything wrong and now your kid is *fat*, don't believe it. All of us do the best job we know how to do at the time. Even your mother and your Great-aunt Mathilda were innocent (although it's sometimes hard to see that). The important thing now is to get that obese child fit. Never mind all the mistakes that got him obese in the first place. It is also time to start getting him in touch with eating slowly and with recognizing what being full feels like, and giving him permission, even encouragement, to take back his power over food and leave something on his plate if he wants to.

THE SLOW CHILD

One of the tragedies of our education system is that it categorizes. It sets standards for where children are supposed to be, physically and mentally, by a given time. It sets these standards according to a norm. These standards are absolutely arbitrary. We lose sight of the fact that they merely represent the majority; we forget that there are supposed to be children on either side of that majority. So the quicker children are judged somehow better and the slower children are judged somehow worse.

A friend of ours has a child with serious learning disabilities. He is one of the most self-confident, outgoing, popular children you'd ever want to meet. Our friend knew from the third week of his life that she was going to have to focus on building self-esteem if he was to survive his disability with any kind of quality. She began building on what he could do. She reinforced every positive little thing she could find. Then she broke down all the difficulties into their doable parts and began constructing positive components there, too.

If you have a slow child, you know the heartbreak and you know that his slowness doesn't make him less lovable, less wonderful, or less your darling. Please know that exercise programs can make an enormous difference to your child. Exercise programs can be slowed down so that the slower child can master them and get wonderful feelings of accomplishment out of them. It is up to parents and teachers to reinforce those positive feelings. If you want your child to improve, praise and consistency are the only means to get from here to there.

Suzy once had a Down's syndrome child in an exercise class. The child's mother brought him to her at three weeks of age. Suzy worked with him once a week; the mother worked with him every day. By the time the child was three months old, he was more advanced than the new children coming into the studio at three months. He did slow down, but he was always much further ahead of other Down's syndrome babies of his age. And he really enjoyed both the exercises and the closeness that exercising one-on-one provided.

Slow children who are given exercises to do gain years in academic improvement. It is one of the things parents can *do* for their children. That's the basis of the Special Olympics.

How to break down a pattern into doable parts

If you want your child to be able to walk in patterns across the floor (to do exercise CE-2, Pigeon and Upright Duck Walk, page 72, for example) the first step is to get him to be able to walk across the floor to the beat of a piece of music. Start with any slow music with a definite beat. Before you add any complications, graduate the walk to increasingly brisk tempos. Make certain your child walks to the beat. Clap your hands in the beginning until he can pick up the beat himself. Be patient.

To teach your child to walk with both feet turned out, start with slowing down the music again. Have him walk across the floor with the right foot turned out. Let him get the feel of the right foot turning out. Now have him walk across the room with the left foot turned out. Again, let him get the feel of the foot turning out, and praise him continually.

Now try the walk with both feet turned out. Be patient and go slowly; there's no face lost if he can't move on. Eventually he will be able to. Just go back to working with one foot at a time and keep practicing. Sometime he'll be able to walk across the room with both feet turned out.

Next you want to teach him to turn his feet in when he walks. Do the same process as you did before, only this time with feet turned in. This walk is more difficult and may take a little longer to achieve.

Once you have achieved both the duck walk and the pigeon walk, it is time for patterning. Patterning is an excellent way to increase brain function as well as coordination. To pattern, have your child walk four steps with feet turned out, then four steps with feet turned in. Keep walking in time to the music. Have him cross the room in this manner.

All of the exercises in this book can be broken down into simple steps this way. If exercises call for hands and feet and that's too much, do the feet first, then the hands. If the exercises call for both feet and that's too much, do one foot and then the other. If the rhythms are too fast, slow them down. Go over and over an exercise slowly, and slowly build speed and complication. The slow child will learn whatever you want him to learn. Be patient, and enjoy the time together.

6

Thinking Positive

Mind over matter is more than just a catchy phrase. More and more, sports professionals are finding that feeding their minds positive statements and beliefs helps them achieve their goals. Children, especially, need to be fed positive information about themselves.

Our children are still being taught that they are wrong if they can't do something. Feeling wrong causes tension, low self-esteem, and fear. Fear interferes with their ability to do correctly whatever it is that they want to do. Children must be taught to concentrate on what they can do at any given time and make it better, instead of concentrating on or worrying about what they can't do.

What teachers do all too often is focus on negative qualities of performance, what they *don't* want to happen. And what happens is that their worst expectations come true. If we continually tell our children what they do wrong, they never get a picture of what is right. All they hear is what makes up their failure, and as a result they have no way to picture success. We have to turn this around.

Your child isn't a professional athlete, and his body doesn't have a complete mental and physical image of how to perform a sport correctly. He lacks a vocabulary of correct movement. For your child, particularly between the ages of five and eleven, games must be broken down into their component parts, and into increments for success. Within the context of every physical activity, sport, and game, each component must be mastered; each mastery is a blueprint for success.

Games are big things for little people to win. For a little person, "winning a game" can be an overwhelming task; winning can even get in the way of winning. But each game is made up of many small parts. A good coach will shift the focus of his team away from winning as the only end in playing and toward achieving success in any one of the component parts of the game. That way, even if a child is able only to keep his eye on the ball during a game, he wins something. Winning becomes possible even within the context of losing.

Major sports figures in America have learned that by focusing on what is *right* in their own performance, they have a better chance of succeeding than if they worry about what they do wrong. Olympic medalists see themselves *in the process* of doing the best of whatever it is they do. They literally program themselves to succeed. This is what we must teach our children. At this point in time, we are still programming most of them to fail (and not only in sports).

Part of the problem in teaching is in our verbal communication habits. Some parents, teachers, and other children know exactly what each child does wrong, and never hesitate to tell him about it. (They also know what they themselves do wrong, and they never hesitate to tell themselves about it.) We still have parents, teachers, and coaches who call children "stupid," "klutz," "jerk," and other terms of negative reinforcement. Kids get called these names even if they make only a simple mistake. Children think this is part of being a child. It must stop.

In order to retrain ourselves and our children to focus on the positive, we have to deprogram years of negative training. An exercise to practice so that this will become possible is the "Something I like about you" exercise.

Start by playing this game with your child several times a day. Say, "Something I like about what you just did is . . ." Be sure you have something in mind when you start that sentence, and then tell him what it is. Things you want to reinforce could be as simple as "I like the way you came into the room." "I like your walk." "I like your smile." "I like what you chose to wear today." There can be something you like in every situation. Teach your child to tell others what he finds nice about them. The child should simply say "Thank you" when you tell him something nice. If your child tells you something nice about you, you should also just say "Thank you." One important note: it isn't necessary for your child to tell you something nice about you if you tell him something nice about him. Compliments are to be received and enjoyed in and of themselves; they aren't a trade-off.

Next get him to tell you what he finds nice about himself, too. Practice telling yourself nice things about yourself. It's not egocentric; it builds self-esteem and promotes achievement and success. Don't worry about your child learning about his negatives; he has ample opportunity in this world to learn the bad things. The thing you want him to learn is the good stuff. Your child can learn about the positive things in life through your example. Both of you will begin to focus on the positive in every situation.

AFFIRMATIONS

Affirmations are another tool for helping kids succeed. Affirmations are positive thoughts that take the place of, and drown out, negative thought. Many people create affirmations that are statements about what they would like to achieve. That doesn't work too well with children. They're a little too literal for that. Instead of trying to fool the mind by saying, "I am now a wonderful batter," over and over again, the child could say, "Every time I'm up, I am getting better at keeping my eye on the ball and following through." That's a little harder to dispute, and it's ultimately what he wants to achieve.

"Keeping the eye on the ball and following through" is good for most ball sports. Find the important component for each activity you want to perfect, and focus your child's attention on what you what to have happen. Focus by talking about how it improves every day, as if the improvement has already begun, not as if the whole thing were an accomplished fact or something that was going to take place some-time in the distant future.

Affirmation doesn't mean saying over and over again, "I will not trip between first and second base." That's an open invitation to trip. Affirmations are positive statements. They can be as nonspecific as repeating, "I will replace every bad thought I have with three good thoughts." It isn't necessary to be more specific than that. It is only important to begin to retrain your habits of focusing. Eventually positive focusing becomes automatic.

The most important thing you can do for your child is to give that child a belief in himself. High self-esteem is a major ingredient for success as an adult. High self-esteem starts with the thoughts one has about oneself in childhood. Affirmations are good tools for implanting such thoughts. The actions that support those thoughts will follow.

Appendix A: Exercises Grouped by Emphasis

Because we've given you a set of programs, your child will be performing a range of exercises daily as part of his routine. If you want to concentrate on anything special, you can locate it here.

ABDOMINALS

The abdominals are a group of muscles that cover the outside of the stomach. They are core muscles on which many sports depend. Abdominals are some of the most important core muscles in the body and contribute significantly to living without back pain in adult life. They are also highly important for women who intend to have children. The strength of the abdominals contributes to quality recovery from childbearing. Healthy, strong abdominals are tremendously important for children who want to participate in sports; things such as follow-through and support are dependent on them.

ABDOMINAL EXERCISES

MIDRIFF AND BACK

We use the muscles at the side of the body to help us with lifting and carrying. It is very important to have strong side-of-the-body muscles to get us through our daily living routines. The midriff exercises are important for figure control, too. A lovely waistline without rubber tires can be developed through midriff exercises.

MIDRIFF AND BACK EXERCISES

BACK

Back exercises break down into two groups: upper back and lower back.

Upper back exercises have two major functions: one is to build strength; the other, to improve posture. Many children, girls in particular, develop round shoulders in their childhood, which can have profound effects on posture in later years. Round shoulders are also implicated in the development of low back pain, because these muscles are connected to the lower back.

Lower back exercises are most important for supporting the body. These muscles, too, are core muscles. They act in opposition to the abdominal muscles and are essential for support and follow-through in sports. Lower back muscles are apt to be weaker than upper back muscles and are more vulnerable to injury. It is vital to get these muscles both strong and flexible.

BACK EXERCISES

SHOULDERS AND ARMS

Shoulders and arms are made beautiful through exercise. Flexibility in the arms and shoulders is essential to sports participation, both to achieve full range of motion and to prevent hyperextension, which might cause injury. Shoulder and arm strength is very poor among American girls and should be encouraged at every opportunity.

SHOULDER AND ARM EXERCISES

HIPS

Hips are major support joints, covering the body area from the outside of the waist to the upper thigh. They don't get exercised outward naturally, but once in a while, to recover from a bad slip, for instance, or to participate in winter sports, you need them immediately. It's important to be sure to exercise them; that way, when you need them they're there for you.

HIP EXERCISES

LEGS

Leg strength is vital for walking, running, and almost all sports participation from skiing to Ping-Pong. Strong, well-rounded legs look beautiful in a pair of shorts. But most important, the legs are regarded as a secondary pump in the cardiovascular system. It is walking and using the legs that facilitate the pumping of the blood uphill toward the heart. Using the legs is essential in your exercise plan.

LEG EXERCISES

FEET AND ANKLES

The feet are your sports foundation. Like flexibility, feet get very little attention in the average sports program. It is assumed that if you are standing up on them they work, yet if we observe the way people use their feet, quite often sports are performed around the inconvenience of feet that don't work too well. We see joggers, in particular, jogging on flat feet, which must be awful for the joints higher up. We see children running with their feet turned out as if to avoid the whole business of feet altogether. These children are not the star athletes their parents may hope they will be. For an edge in athletics, paying attention to foot exercises is vitally important, and you can pretty well bet that your children are not going to get these exercises in an average school program. Do them here.

FEET AND ANKLE EXERCISES

Appendix B: Exercises by Category

KRAUS-WEBER MINIMUM MUSCULAR FITNESS TEST

OPTIMUM FITNESS TEST

FLEXIBILITY

Hamstring Muscles: As we have explained in other parts of this book, hamstring flexibility is vital for lower back health, for sports participation, and for safety in sports. Hamstring flexibility breaks down into three major areas, and combinations of them: Achilles tendon, back of the legs, and buttocks to lower back. Just as it is important to see the hamstring as a whole, it is also important to see it in its component parts. A child who has excellent lower back flexibility may do irreparable damage to an Achilles tendon in a hyperextension injury without hamstring flexibility.

Upper Body: Flexibility is not just about the hamstring muscles, however. Exercises such as the Feet Apart, Bottoms Up, and Chest Stretch (page 77) incorporate the hamstring muscles, upper back, chest, and arms. Note, too, the back stretches when doing Sitting, Feet Together, Forward Pulse (page 37). As you become accustomed to all your flexibility exercises, you will know exactly which parts of the body they stretch.

FLEXIBILITY EXERCISES

WEIGHTS

Again, weights should be used judiciously because of the possibility of stress on young muscles. Weights enhance the program by cutting down on the number of repetitions needed to make an exercise work. But it is vitally important for you and your child to remember that he cannot add bulk before he reaches puberty. He can define his muscles, but he cannot make them look like the Hulk's. (At puberty there is a specific enzyme released that makes it possible to build bulk; before puberty he will only frustrate himself and run the risk of injury and loss of self-esteem if he tries to add bulk.) The ideal for the child using weights should be long, lean muscles and good flexibility.

If your child likes to use weights, be sure you insist on a strong flexibility program as well, by using the flexibility exercises interspersed in the weight program.

WEIGHT EXERCISES

RESISTANCE

Resistance exercises don't work on a specific part of the body, but enhance the exercise as weights do and are part of a more advanced program.

RESISTANCE EXERCISES

EQUIPMENT

The jump rope is one of the best all-around pieces of exercise equipment. It is effective for body coordination, eye-hand coordination, and aerobics. Best of all, it's cheap and readily available. There's no reason why every child in America can't have a jump rope. Dowels, tubing, and beach balls are readily available as well and make programs more interesting.

Gymnastic equipment, in particular, makes exercising more fun. It does several things: it exercises the children, and it creates goals to shoot for—walking isn't half as challenging as walking across a balance beam. While some of these pieces of equipment seem to contribute to a child's sense of balance, on a more subtle level they are teaching the child physical self-assurance.

EQUIPMENT EXERCISES

GYMNASTICS EQUIPMENT EXERCISES

EYE-HAND COORDINATION

Eye-hand coordination games and exercises are essential for children who want to participate successfully in school sports programs. They are valuable for everyone, and we absolutely encourage parents to make sure their children develop skills in these areas.

EYE-HAND COORDINATION EXERCISES

COORDINATION AND ENDURANCE

These exercise are slightly different from aerobic endurance exercises, though not too far off the beam. Performed across a yard or living room, they can raise the heart rate significantly. These exercises are fun, they can be part of games and sports, and they will significantly exercise the muscles used in gross muscle movements. They are very important for those children who are interested in the kinds of sports that require more than just straight running: soccer, football, basketball, lacrosse, tennis, squash, and racquetball, to name a few. All benefit from coordination and endurance exercises.

COORDINATION AND ENDURANCE EXERCISES

Appendix C: Results of Follow-up Study

In 1986 we conducted a follow-up study using the Kraus-Weber Minimum Muscular Fitness Test on nearly three thousand schoolchildren in Rye, New York; Poughkeepsie, New York; and Bethel, Vermont, the three cities in which Mother conducted her landmark study in 1952. We were happy to find some improvement in the success rate in all three schools. It certainly wasn't what it ought to be, but it was better than it could have been.

In the 1950s only 26 percent of the children entering the Bethel, Vermont, school failed the Kraus-Weber Test. This figure contrasted favorably with the entry-level figures for both Rye, New York (56 percent), and Poughkeepsie, New York (58 percent). Today Bethel still does better on an entry level than Rye and Poughkeepsie: 50 percent of its kindergarten-age children cannot pass, compared to Rye at 73 percent and Poughkeepsie at 59.6 percent.

This means that the sedentary lifestyle has brought rural America more in line with the poor findings in urban and suburban America, and we can no longer count on the rural population to improve the statistics nationally. That's not a great finding.

In 1952 the physical education programs did not have an impact at all on the statistics. Kids entered school at 26 percent, 56 percent, and 58 percent, they got worse around age eleven, and they left school at 26 percent, 56 percent, and 58 percent. Things have improved in that regard in all three schools. We saw marked improvement in both Bethel and Rye between kindergarten and first grade. None of the schools failed Kraus-Weber by more than an overall average of 46.3

percent after kindergarten-level.* We saw great differences in programs, and great differences in testing results. We learned beyond a shadow of a doubt that if you have a good program, kids can become fit in school.

We found that where the old-fashioned game-oriented programs remained, the high failure rates persisted. Where a new type of program—one of physical fitness rather than physical education—has been instituted, things were much better.

We found a school with a marvelous physical fitness program (notice we said physical fitness and not physical education; it's key). Rye, New York, has created a landmark program for its student body. The program proved that physical educators, given support from the school board and the community and the mandate to do the job they have been hired to do, have the knowledge, training, skill, and desire to make a real difference. It proved that it does not take vast expenditures to accomplish a good program. It takes a clear understanding of a different end product.

WHAT RYE DID

Five years earlier, after trying very hard to change their program with the help of outside consultants, Coach Lou Gallo and his staff looked at their physical education program and knew it hadn't succeeded. They made the decision that for it to be effective they would have to stop relying on programs from outside experts. They decided they could effectively shift their own program only if they did it from the inside. They decided that they had to take charge and take responsibility for changing their own program in order to make it work.

With this in mind, they contacted Dr. William G. Anderson at Columbia University, who became their *guide*. When we talked to Dr. Anderson, he couldn't stress enough the Rye faculty's responsibility for its own program. Again and again, he stated that Columbia's function had been simply to show the Rye staff what was possible within the context of what they already knew and that the staff had taken it from there. That's very important: *The first rule of forming any kind of fitness program is to have the staff, from the bottom up, develop the program themselves, so that they have a vested interest in its success and are comfortable teaching it.*

Next Rye decided to *agree on a common outcome for its program, one which would have the kind of a result that would be difficult to*

---

* We think it's important to note that these statistics don't show the dramatic improvement from multiple to single failures. Kraus-Weber is only pass/fail. Fail any part of the test, and it counts as a test failure. However, the shift from multiple to single failures is significant in all three schools, and that should be mentioned. It should also be mentioned that the thing that was consistently failed was flexibility. And flexibility is notably lacking from *all programs—in school and most other programs—in America.*

argue with. They decided they would focus their program on cardio-respiratory health. They would reduce the risks of heart disease in the student body. They would teach lifetime fitness. To do this, they knew they had to shift their physical education program from games to exercise. *Physical education programs are weakened in direct proportion to the amount of time devoted to playing games versus exercising.*

To accomplish this monumental task, they decided they would change the name of the course they were teaching from physical education to physical fitness. That was the most profound decision they could have made. It totally redefined the mandate of the Physical Education Department. *If you teach physical education, you teach a broad spectrum of game skills. If you teach physical fitness, you prepare children's bodies to participate in a broad spectrum of games, which skills you might also teach.* The name change was highly significant and totally successful.

The staff decided that it couldn't change everything overnight, so it kept its existing high school and middle school program and focused its attention on the elementary school. Later, when it had a population that had been through the elementary school program, it introduced the physical fitness components to the middle and high schools. It was because of this continuity that we saw continual improvement from kindergarten through twelfth grade.

The teachers recognized that the children loved games best of all, which is the problem with a shift of this nature. They determined to remedy this by including aerobic games and game components in their program. Using a book that shows how to change stand-around games to active games, they adjusted their curriculum so that kids simply didn't stand around. An example is Garbage Ball, a variation on volleyball: the children are taught to bat balls back and forth as in volleyball, but five balls instead of one are given to each side. The team that wins is the team with the least number of balls on its side of the court at the end of the time period. Needless to say, everybody moves.

They also introduced a twelve-minute aerobics warm-up at the beginning of each class. The warm-up includes running around the gym twice, fifteen side-to-side slides in each direction, fifteen jump-rope jumps, fifteen bent-knee sit-ups, fifteen push-ups, fifteen spike jumps, and fifteen balls hit into the eye of a target. All of this is done to music.

Someone on the staff came up with the idea of clubs. An example is the Ten-Mile Club (see page 138). An area around the school was measured into quarter miles, and the children were urged to use their recess to run. Each of them had record cards, and when a child had run a quarter mile in the presence of an adult, his card was signed. When a child had accumulated ten miles' worth of signatures, he was awarded a prize and became a member of the Ten-Mile Club.

The classroom teachers were encouraged to participate, too. They were urged to walk during their breaks. The kids were delighted to know that their teachers were participating in the school's new fitness program. It was great for the teachers and it supported the kids.

There was an amazing effect on the Rye girls. Although New York State has legislated that girls will be treated exactly like boys in physical education classes, that's honored more by presenting equal course material than by encouraging direct competition (particularly in middle schools, where boys and girls have "discovered" each other). The effect is supposed to be separate but equal education, and it hasn't worked particularly well. In most schools the girls never get a chance to go head-to-head against the boys. They never get the message that boys are just people and that girls can compete and win. In the elementary schools in Rye the girls regularly compete with the boys, and the results are very exciting. The girls learned that they could compete as equals or betters. The staff mentioned how pleasantly surprised they were at the difference between the girls' performance before the program was started and their performance once the new program had been in effect for a while.

The only area not addressed by the new Rye program was flexibility, and that was what we found when we tested. By fifth grade, 85 percent of the Rye elementary school children could pass the President's AAHPER Physical Fitness Test (flexibility is not a part of that test), whereas 54.8 percent passed the Kraus-Weber Test. Of the twenty-four children who failed, twenty-three failed only one test, and in twenty-two cases, the one test they failed was flexibility. Of the twenty-two who failed in flexibility, fifteen were boys.

MOVING THE PROGRAM UP

When Rye had a population that had been through the elementary school program for a few years, they expanded the program upward. The changes that were made in the middle school and high school programs were highly significant. Many American children are having coordination difficulties by the time they reach their middle school years, but Rye the children are in good shape.

OTHER INCENTIVES RYE ADDED

In Rye, not only is physical fitness a requirement for graduation, but even more important, the physical education grades are factored into the grade average every semester. Each student is graded on individual performance against his own talent. It is quite possible to get an A in Rye if you are a klutz who puts in a great deal of effort. It is equally possible to get a D if you are skilled and do not put in effort. We didn't see much potential for the latter—everyone appeared to be having too much fun.

In Rye, fun in Physical Fitness is the watchword of the department. The program recognizes that if fitness is going to be part of lifetime living, it can't be agony.

Attention has been taken off uniforms, class preparedness, and attendance. Although we saw teachers taking attendance, they never stopped the class to do so. When you consider that classes in school are forty minutes long, ten to fifteen minutes for changing and five to ten minutes for attendance take a huge bite out of movement time. We saw the kids in gym clothes, but we did not see children in uniform. Rye does not include hygiene in its physical education requirements either; it stresses *physical fitness,* cardiorespiratory physical fitness to be exact, and it sticks to what it has defined as its goal. We found that that wasn't possible in some of the other schools.

The Physical Education Department found that this new goal was effective in eliciting the help and cooperation of the parents. Parents tended to be willing to excuse their children for almost any reason when it came to learning game skills. They were often slow on getting sneakers into school. When they learned that their children's future cardiorespiratory health was what was the underpinning of this new physical fitness course, there was a dramatic shift: parents wholeheartedly supported the program.

Rye found that there was a similar support shift in the Guidance Department when it came to scheduling. Physical education has traditionally been the stepchild of most schools. But supporting the cardiorespiratory health of the student body is another story. Scheduling, particularly on the high school level, where it's difficult, reflected the support of the new program.

The Rye administrators talked to local doctors and asked for their cooperation in getting kids back into class sooner if they had been out because of illness or accident. If a student had a broken arm, they asked the doctor to specify what activities he definitely should be excluded from and what he could still do. Since there was nothing wrong with his legs, he might run or exercycle or even participate in an aerobic dance class. There is no such thing as a blanket excuse anymore, unless, of course, there is a blanket reason.

Kids who are excused from classes can no longer use their physical fitness time as an extra study hall. They are given articles to read about the games that are currently being played, and take a test or write a paper about what they have read at the end of their excused period. This seems to be a true motivation to get off the sick list quickly.

Intramurals were dropped in Rye. It was found that they limited the number of children who could participate in sports after school. Instead, the Physical Fitness Department allowed the aerobic games the kids loved to play to spill over into their after-school activities. One of the more telling statements we heard in another, less successful program came while we were watching about forty happy boys dunking balls into baskets. "These kids would do this all day *if we'd let them.*"

Experts in specific sports within the department broke their sports down into parts and made games that were aerobic out of those parts. Basketball became a game of "21," a fast-paced game involving shooting and guarding baskets without the limitations of breaking into teams. This way, instead of only a few children playing at any one time, all of them play all period long. It also enhances their skills so that those who *do* want to play continuously improve without taking time away from those who don't. Rye has many nets and many basketballs, and all the kids play all period long.

We have no way of knowing how expensive this program is in comparison to other programs. We do know that there was a substantial increase in equipment such as balls and jump ropes, equipment that is neither particularly expensive nor fancy. Instead of five basketballs, they had thirty. Instead of ten jump ropes, they had a hundred. This way all the children got to move all the time.

One of the most important factors of the Rye program is variety. In any semester the middle- and high-school-age children choose five activities from eight different possibilities. That way, even if one or two of them aren't favorites, the kids are bound to like something. Choices range from aerobic exercising to a Bruce Jenner tape, to weight lifting, basketball, tennis, and badminton. Coach Lou Gallo, the director of this program, gives an automatic A to anyone who can beat him at badminton; badminton at Rye is cutthroat, which sounds almost like a contradiction in terms!

The program works.